Francis Thynne's
Emblemes and Epigrames.

BERLIN: ASHER & CO., 53 MOHRENSTRASSE.
NEW YORK: C. SCRIBNER & CO.; LEYPOLDT & HOLT.
PHILADELPHIA: J. B. LIPPINCOTT & CO.

Emblemes and Epigrames.

Psal:

Quum defecerit virtus mea,

ne derelinquas me,

Domine.

[A.D. 1600, BY

FRANCIS THYNNE,

LANCASTER HERALD, AUTHOR OF "ANIMADVERSIONS ON SPEGHT'S EDITION OF CHAUCERS WORKES 1598," ETC.]

EDITED BY

F. J. FURNIVALL, M.A., CAMB.

LONDON:
PUBLISHED FOR THE EARLY ENGLISH TEXT SOCIETY,
BY N. TRÜBNER & CO., 57 & 59, LUDGATE HILL.

OXFORD
UNIVERSITY PRESS

Great Clarendon Street, Oxford ox2 6DP
United Kingdom

Oxford University Press is a department of the University of Oxford.
It furthers the University's objective of excellence in research, scholarship,
and education by publishing worldwide. Oxford is a registered trade mark of
Oxford University Press in the UK and in certain other countries

© The Early English Text Society 1876

The moral rights of the authors have been asserted

Database right Oxford University Press (maker)

First Edition published in 1876

All rights reserved. No part of this publication may be reproduced,
stored in a retrieval system, or transmitted, in any form or by any means,
without the prior permission in writing of Oxford University Press,
or as expressly permitted by law, or under terms agreed with the appropriate
reprographics rights organization. Enquiries concerning reproduction
outside the scope of the above should be sent to the Rights Department,
Oxford University Press, at the address above

You must not circulate this book in any other form
and you must impose this same condition on any acquirer

Published in the United States of America by Oxford University Press
198 Madison Avenue, New York, NY 10016, United States of America

British Library Cataloguing in Publication Data
Data available

Library of Congress Cataloging in Publication Data
Data available

Original Series, 64

ISBN 978-0-85-991835-0

FOREWORDS.

THIS Text owes its printing, not to its own poetical merits, but to its adding somewhat to our knowledge of Francis Thynne,—the Chaucer-commentator, the author of the *Animadversions* of 1599 on Speght's *Chaucer*,—of whom and whose works I have given such a full account in my re-edition of those *Animadversions* for the Society's Reprints[1].

The *Emblemes* and *Epigrames* are both dull and poor; but they contain the wife-worrid Thynne's opinions on wives—who're always necessary evils, the best is bad; who're good when they die of old age, better when they die after some time during your life, and best when they die at once (p. 59);—his lines on some of the friends of himself and his patron Sir Thomas Egerton, Lord Chancellor, " in those yonger yeares when Lincolns Inn societie did linke vs all in one cheyne of Amitie "—Thomas Valence[2], p. 47; (Francis) Meringe[3], p. 61; Browne, p. 62;—a note of an old London inn, 'the Rose within Newgate', p. 75, where friends then gatherd and chatted; a few illustrations of Shakspere—'glasse vessells for banquettinge are dailie had in pryse', for Falstaff's 'Glasses, glasses is the only

---

[1] This re-edition is more than four times the size of our 1st edition, and contains the only known fragment of the *Pilgrims Tale*. Members can have it at half-price, 5s., with 6d. more for postage.

[2] See Notes, p. 101.

[3] "Among the Lincoln's Inn Admissions, the names of John Browne and Francis Meringe both appear in the list, 23 January, 4 Philip and Mary, A.D. 1558. There is also a Thomas Browne, admitted 13 Octr., 3 Eliz. A.D. 1561. I observe in the list of 3 Eliz. the name of William Goldbourne, admitted Febr. 15, with the names of John Browne and Thomas Egerton as his manucaptors."—Martin Doyle, Steward. The names of Waterhouse, p. 60; Stukelie, p. 71; Willford, p. 73; Garrett, p. 75; Humfrie Waldroun, p. 76; Burrell, p. 77; Eldrington, p. 94, do not seem to be in the Lincoln's Inn lists, so far as Mr Doyle's searches have extended.

drinking[1]', 2 *Hen. IV*, II. i. 151; 'Dictinian Diana', for Holofernes's 'Dictynna, goodman Dull', *Love's Lab. Lost*, IV. ii. 37;—an opinion, interesting for Bacon's case, of a Judge's friend, writing to the highest Judge in the land, showing that bribery of Judges was an openly recognizd matter[2] here in England; and lastly, a set of mentions of, or poems to, the English writers whom Francis Thynne honourd—Chaucer (though Lydgate's *Temple of Glass* is wrongly assignd to him on the authority of Sir John Thynne's MS still at Longleat[3]), p. 62, 71, 77, 3; Spenser (on 'Spencers Fayrie Queene'), p. 71; Gascoigne (his Steele Glasse), p. 62, l. 11; Arthur Golding, p. 77, l. 16; Camden (on Mr Camden's *Britania*), p. 93, 95; and Leland, p. 95. To me, an Egham man, the 'Gallopinge' poem on p. 80 is interesting, from its mention of Hounslow Heath, which I've so often driven over, and where my father, riding many years ago, was accosted one evening by a highwayman, who was shot a few minutes after, by Lord Stowell.

The motive of Francis Thynne in presenting his autograph poems to his patron, Sir Thomas Egerton, was doubtless, gratitude, both in its ordinary meaning of 'thankfulness for past benefits', and in its extraordinary sense of 'a keen sense of future favours'. It is pretty clear from Thynne's 13th Embleame, 'Liberalitie', and his 61st, 'Benefitts', that he expected Egerton to give him something,—hard cash, no doubt—and that soon, for he adds the reminder,

.. hee gives twice, that quicklie and with speed
bestowes his guift to serve our present need.—l. 47-8.

In the Ivy poem, p. 82, l. 5, we get a glimpse of Francis Thynne's ivy-coverd 'howse in Clerkenwell Greene', then a pleasant suburban

[1] See the capital bit on this in Harrison's *Description of England*, p. 147 of my edition for the New Shakspere Society; and Stafford's *Conceipte*, p. 51, New Sh. Soc.

[2] Soe the old Iudge, once fullie fraughte
    with guiftes and briberie,
Will not be easilie ledd by guiftes
    to wrest the lawes awrye.
But hee that commeth new in place,
    and thirsteth after gould,
Or his Iuditiall office buyes,
    with him there is noe hould;
for hee that buies, is forct to sell;
    and new corrupted Iudge
Takes all and more; and, for reward,
    is made a sinfull drudge.

[3] See Mr Bradshaw's note in my edition of F. Thynne's *Animadversions*, p. 30.

village, in which he finally settl'd down, and where—of drink and gout, as is suppos'd,—he died in 1604. Whether his 71st Epigram, 'The Courte and Cuntrey', p. 88—91, represents his own case and opinions I cannot tell: its arguments are the regular stock ones of the time; and I can hardly think that he, living at Clerkenwell, and going in to the Heralds' College regularly to his work, could pretend to be a countryman as oppos'd to a Londoner.

The Text is printed from Thynne's autograph MS, belonging to Lord Ellesmere, who has been kind enough to lend it me to print, for which I thank him much. The italics in words are expansions of MS contractions; words wholly in italics are those written by Thynne in a larger hand than the rest of his lines.

My thanks are due, and are hereby tenderd, to Mr Martin Doyle, the Steward of Lincoln's Inn, for searching the early Admission-books for me; to Colonel Chester, for his identification of Thomas Valence; to Mr P. A. Daniel for his many kind hints and notes; and to Mr W. G. Stone for his Index and notes.

The Arboretum, Leamington,
   Good Friday, April 14, 1876.

CONTENTS.

EMBLEMES.

(1) Pietie and Impietie, p. 5.
(2) Vertue should not be condempned for one smale imperfection, p. 6.
(3) Temperance abateth fleshlie Delightes, p. 6.
(4) Death and Cupid, p. 7.
(5) Art, the antidote against fortune, p. 8.
(6) Labour quencheth Lecherie, p. 8.
(7) Fortune, p. 9.
(8) Bryberie, p. 10.
(9) Immortallitie of the Sowle, p. 11.
(10) Sotted loue, p. 12.
(11) Pride, p. 12.
(12) Patience, p. 13.
(13) Liberalitie, p. 14.
(14) Vertue of Herbes, p. 16.
(15) Wine, p. 16.
(16) Mann, p. 17.
(17) Witt, p. 18.
(18) The subiect (follows the Prince, as the Heliotrope does the Sun), p. 18.
(19) Diligence obtayneth Riches, p. 20.
(20) Vsurie, p. 20.
(21) Myrtilus Sheilde, p. 21.
(22) Vayne Ostentations, p. 21.
(23) Losse of hurtfull thinges is gayne, p. 22.
(24) Internall vertues are best, p. 23.
(25) Threates of the inferior to be contemned, p. 23.
(26) Philosophie, p. 24.
(27) Societie, p. 25.
(28) Counsell and vertue subdue deceipfull Persons, p. 25.
(29) Pleasures to be eschewed, p. 26.
(30) Vnitinge of Contraries make sound Iudgement, p. 27.
(31) Reuenge, p. 27.
(32) Peace, p. 28.
(33) Pouertie, p. 29.
(34) Syluer worlde, p. 29.
(35) Enuye, p. 29.
(36) Our terme or limit of life not remoueable, p. 30.
(37) God slowlie punisheth, p. 31.
(38) Dull witts, p. 32.
(39) The wretched not to be Doblie greiued, p. 32.

CONTENTS. EMBLEMES. EPIGRAMES.

(40) Noe impuritie in heauen, p. 33.
(41) Honor and rewarde nourisheth artes, p. 34.
(42) Eloquence, p. 34.
(43) Art cannot take awaye the vice of nature, p. 35.
(44) Fortune, p. 35.
(45) Ganymede, p. 36.
(46) Eloquent wisdome, p. 36.
(47) Poetrye, p. 37.
(48) Ensignes of the Clergye, p. 37.
(49) Flatterers, p. 39.
(50) Our betters or enemies not to be prouoked with wordes, p. 39.
(51) Wisdome and Strength are to be Ioyned, p. 40.
(52) The Meane (between extremes), p. 40.
(53) Not to climbe ouer highe, p. 41.
(54) Monument of a harlott, p. 41.
(55) Earthlie mindes, p. 42.
(56) The olde Testament, p. 43.
(57) Sophistrie, p. 43.
(58) Ingratitude, p. 45.
(59) Children in youth to be framed, p. 45.
(60) Of the same, p. 46.
(61) Benefitts, p. 46.
(62) Prodigalitie, p. 47.
(63) To m^r Thomas Valence, p. 47.
(64) Strangers more freindlie to vs then our owne kinde and kindred, p. 49.

EPIGRAMES.

(1) The Armes of England, p. 53.
(2) Crisopeia, p. 53.
(3) Vpon the armed Statue of Venus, p. 54.
(4) Sundrie and strange effectes of wyne, p. 54.
(5) Contemninge, p. 56.
(6) What maketh menn forgett themselues, p. 56.
(7) Thinges not to be recalled, p. 56.
(8) The vnapt not to be forced to learninge, p. 57.
(9) The waye to gett and keepe frendes, p. 57.
(10) Of Stumblinge, p. 58.
(11) First guestes at a feaste, p. 58.
(12) When a wife is badd, worse, and worst. When she is good, better, and beste, p. 59.
(13) A Puritane, p. 59.
(14) Of heauie and light, p. 59.
(15) Waterhowse, p. 60.
(16) A preist which knewe not anie letter, p. 60.

(17) The hedd and the tayle, p. 60.
(18) Cause of a deere yeare, p. 61.
(19) Pinkes, p. 61.
(20) Shoinge, p. 62.
(21) Glasses, p. 62.
(22) One assured he was elected, p. 63.
(23) Cham (Ham), p. 63.
(24) Fayth, p. 63.
(25) Cuttinge of tyme, p. 63.
(26) A tench and a wench, p. 64.
(27) Whoe are happie, p. 64.
(28) Linguistes, p. 65.
(29) Drinkinge, p. 65.
(30) Enuye, p. 66.
(31) Mann must provide for bodie and sowle, p. 66.
(32) Mongers, p. 67.
(33) Tyme, p. 68.
(34) Receipts and expenses, p. 68.
(35) Counterfetts deuoure the whole world, p. 69.
(36) That one thinge Produceth annother, p. 69.
(37) A longe nose, p. 70.
(38) Spencers Fayrie Queene, p. 71.
(39) Martine, p. 71.
(40) Vsurers, p. 71.
(41) Grace, p. 72.
(42) Cardinge, p. 72.
(43) Reelinge, p. 73.
(44) A Rose, p. 73.
(45) Sowinge, p. 73.

(46) Woodcocks, p. 74.
(47) Kissinge, p. 74.
(48) White heares, p. 75.
(49) Cutters, p. 76.
(50) The deceased Pretor, p. 76.
(51) To Humfrie Waldronn, p. 76.
(52) Fortune, p. 77.
(53) To his freind Burrell, p. 77.
(54) Issues, p. 78.
(55) Mariage, p. 78.
(56) Sweete mouthes, p. 79.
(57) Fooles, p. 79.
(58) Gallopinge, p. 80.
(59) Churches, p. 81.
(60) Menn before Adame, p. 81.
(61) Iuye, p. 82.
(62) Iestinge, p. 82.
(63) Honor, p. 83.
(64) Temperance, p. 83.
(65) Doinge nothinge, p. 85.
(66) Astrologers, p. 85.
(67) The herbe *filius ante Patrem*, p. 86.
(68) Monstrous Childe, p. 86.
(69) A godly Mann, p. 87.
(70) Kindred, p. 88.
(71) The Courte and Cuntrey, p. 88.
(72) The number 1, 2, 3, 4, p. 92.
(73) Mr Camdens Britania, p. 93.
(74) Solomons witt, p. 94.
(75) Leylandes rightefull ghost. p. 95.
(76) Quiet and Rest, p. 96.

INDEX OF FIRST LINES.

EMBLEMES.

		PAGE
(8) After his Fathers funerall, when as Tiberius went	...	10
(33) As fishe *Remora* staies the Shipp	... ...	29
(44) As goulden Sonne doth worke from out the Skye	...	35
(60) As tender whelpe, whome natures skill hath taught	...	46
(10) Autoritie and *Loue* will scarce agree	... .	12
(16) Behould, mann is the litle world	... ...	17
(53) *Bellerephon*, which ruld without offence	... ...	41
(30) Comforting *Ceres* Ioynd with hopps of bitter taste	...	27
(31) *Dianiane* dogge, with blinde furie inflamed	... ...	27
(6) *Dictinian Diana*, which of *Phœbus* borroweth lighte	...	8
(51) Doe tell, rude verse, why that pure virginn fayre	...	40
(15) ffayne wouldst thow know wherfore the god	... ...	16
(29) ffonde *Paris*, in vnbridled age doth chuse	... ...	26
(36) ffrom neck it hath the humane shape, the rest a piller stone		30
(9) In former age, the *Ethnikes*, false gods servinge	...	11
(59) In yongest yeares, when will and strength doe want	...	45
(26) Ioues sonne, the valiant *Hercules*	... ...	24
(64) My loved frend, and lovinge therwithall	... ...	49
(63) My Valence, to thy learned vewe this skillesse vers I sende		47
(17) Nothing more smooth then artificiall glasse	... ...	18
(5) On rolling ball doth fickle fortune stande	... ...	8
(32) *Pluto*, the god of worldlie wealth	... ...	28
(23) Producinge earth inrich'd, makes rich againe	... ...	22
(57) *Saturns* daughter, and *Ioue* his Iealious wife ...	...	43

INDEX OF FIRST LINES. EMBLEMES. xiii

		PAGE
(41)	Shewe mee, sweete muse, why thow and all the rest ...	34
(42)	Some learned menn affirme by abstruce skill	34
(50)	*Strymonian* Cranes, which by their ayerie flight ...	39
(24)	Sweet tasting aple, which this faire virginn beares ...	23
(47)	The artificiall Scale composd of gould	37
(39)	The birde of *Ioue*, the Eagle of flight most free ...	32
(40)	The blinded boye, which with his peircinge darts ...	33
(38)	The cheife of gods, the mightie *Ioue*	32
(62)	The craftie Fox, with longe and bushye tayle ...	47
(52)	The *Daulian Philomell*, whose warblinge voice ...	40
(21)	The famous souldier, *Myrtilus* the Knighte	21
(4)	The hatefull *Death* Ioynd to the *God of loue*	7
(43)	The healthfull bathe which daielie wee doe see ...	35
(2)	The heavenlie pallas of Celestiall skye	6
(25)	The melitane dogge, bredd onlie for delight	23
(35)	The mightie *Ioue* from highest heaven did sende ...	29
(11)	The morrall *Seneca*, whose penn intreatinge matters graue	12
(56)	The Oke, bearing a corne, *Ioues* sacred tree	43
(12)	The patient *Socrates*, true mirror of our life	13
(27)	The purple Rose which first *Damasco* bredd	25
(7)	There is a birde which takes the name of Paradise the faire	9
(49)	There is a kinde of men, whome hell hath bredd ...	39
(34)	The sacred Crowne adorning curled hayre	29
(61)	The silver Moone, *Diana* Virgine bright	46
(19)	The simple Cock, that with a hungrie minde	20
(58)	The stam'ringe Cuckooe, whose lewd voice doth greeve	45
(18)	The statlie flower that faire rich India yeldes	19
(55)	The statelie Stagg, whose hornes threaten the skye ...	42
(46)	The talking byrd, which gloriously is cladd	36
(28)	The valiant knight whome *Perseus* wife did love ...	25
(20)	The wealthie mann with blessings great indued ...	20
(3)	Thow *Cithereane Venus*, I would knowe	6
(48)	Thow doest demaund of me	37
(22)	Wee dailie see the fruitfull *Phœbus* fier	21
(37)	What doth the waightie millstone meane	31
(1)	When false *Synon*, with tongue of guilefull tale ...	5

		PAGE
(14) Whilste prudent *Epidaure*, the learned leeche	...	16
(54) Whose tombe is this? whose bones doth this contayne		41
(13) Why doe these virginns faire, the *Graces* three	...	14
(45) Yea, impure mindes whom vncleane lusts defile	...	36

EPIGRAMES.

(26) A Catholike and a Protestant were frendlie sett at meate		64
(65) A Crabbed Cobler, and his slothfull wife	... ...	85
(37) A knight that should with curtesie a ladie entertayne		70
(6) Alluring bewtie, with her cristall face ...	... ...	56
(41) A man of lewd living all vertue sett at naught	...	72
(32) A messe of mongers on *Holborne hill* ...	... ...	67
(56) A noble Earle, to vertue allwaies bent	... ...	79
(33) An Auncient knight of ffee and of renowne	... ...	68
(27) *Antomedon* the *Greeke Poet* doth tell ...	... ...	64
(76) As wearie bodie doth restore his strength with rest	...	96
(48) At the Rose within Newgate, ther frendlie did meete		75
(34) A tutor, gluttinous and prodigall	... ...	68
(67) A vertuous Ladie, skilfull herbaliste ...	... ...	86
(52) Blinde Fortune, with her fonde and sencelesse sence	...	77
(13) Dame *Lais* is a puritane by religion	... ...	59
(55) Deepe witted menn, b'experience haue contrived	...	78
(68) Did Learned *Ouid* live, with poetrie divine	... ...	86
(3) ffayre *Venus*, tell whye dost thow Armor beare	...	54
(74) ffreind *Eldrington*, thow art as wise ...	... ...	94
(19) Friend *Meering*, I deeme you smell verie sweete	...	61
(58) ffrom Windsore ridinge, to the statelie towne ...	...	80
(9) Fyne witts, much art, sweet tongues, and flatterie	...	57
(20) Good Browne, thow doest complaine with heavie cheere		62
(60) Good *Moses* (which didst write by sprite of God)	...	81
(16) Good zealous preist, thy hart more than thy skill	...	60
(17) Great was the glorious fame, most worthie knight	...	60
(69) He is a godlie mann, that doth with tongue and minde		87

INDEX OF FIRST LINES. EPIGRAMES.

		PAGE
(46) He is as wise as a Woodcock, all wee doe see		74
(57) Hee was not wise, his witt hath him deceyved	...	79
(23) In all the course of thy vnhappie yeares		63
(49) Iack, I here thow hast leaft thine ould trade ...	...	76
(43) Iohn, thy wife, to live doth take great payne	...	73
(42) *Kate* is a good huswife, as all men saye		72
(66) Malevolent *Saturne*, vnhappie starr		85
(39) Menn say thow art call'd the Rich Martine		71
(2) My dolefull muse, bewayle in mournefull rimes	...	53
(12) My frend, yf that my Iudgement do not fayle	...	59
(71) My yonge and youthfull yeares		88
(72) One simple thinge cann nothinge worke		92
(24) Our Saviour *Christ*, with words of greife complayned		63
(14) Philosophers were fooles, that taught of ould		59
(38) Renowmed Spencer, whose heavenlie sprite		71
(40) Stukelie the vsurer is dead, and bid vs all farwell ...		71
(45) Sweete flowers growe when gardeners sowes the seed ...		73
(59) The Aunchient *Saxons* did full Christianlie		81
(11) The buzzinge flye which falls in everie thinge	...	58
(25) The Curious gardiner, with his cruell Shires		63
(4) The drunken menn, whome gluttonie doth fill	...	54
(31) The fairest Creature which the heavenlie hand	...	66
(29) The first delightinge draught		65
(36) The frutefull peace begetts desired plentie		69
(63) The glorious Queene, honor, desir'd of all		83
(64) The heroike vertues Cardinall		83
(73) The holie licor, whose mysteries divine		93
(54) The Ioyfull mother brings forth manie faire yssues ...		78
(35) The kinge deuoures the husbandman		69
(53) The loathed povertie still shall thee feede		77
(10) The prowde horse that treades with statelie pace ...		58
(1) The sacred Lyon of *Iudeas* princelie lyne		53
(7) The stone once cast out of the hand or slinge ...		56
(21) The sundrie sort of glasses which art doth put in vre		62
(61) Thow Bacchus plant, which allwaies greene dost springe		82
(18) Thow fondlie askest me, as though I were a god ...		61

		PAGE
(22)	Thow greatlie bragst how that thow art assur'd	63
(30)	Thow monster of mankinde, obscurer of good name ...	66
(47)	Three pleasant gentlemen vpon the waye	74
(62)	Three things there be which maie susteyne noe Ieste ...	82
(50)	Thy vertue, not thy vice; faith, not dissembling speech	76
(8)	To *Salamanca* yf thow send an Asse ...	57
(28)	Twoe gentlemen at meate by enterchaunge	65
(75)	What *Endore* phytonesse, what envious hart ...	95
(5)	Whoe doeth contempne the worlds fond vanitie	56
(70)	Why kneele you heere, faire Ladies, thus amased	88
(44)	Willford, thow lovest a pleasant Rose verie well	73
(15)	With milder sport, and not with bitter speech	60
(51)	Yf reasons worthie minde prescribe this reede	76

To the right honorable his Singuler
good Lord, Sir Thomas Egerton,
Knight, Lord Keper of
the greate Seale.

IT hath byn, my verie good Lord, a thinge allwaies vsed (and therfore to be pardoned, since custome maketh one other nature, and the Lawe sayth, *Comunis error facit ius*) that as well the learned, throughe the height of their witts, as the vnlearned, through the desire to houlde the course of the worlde, haue delivered their conceites to the viewe of all menn, for as sayth *Perseus :*
   Scribimus indocti doctique poemata passim.
A thinge trulie verefied in mee, whoe, like blinde Bayarde, as an owle amongst birdes, am com vppon the stage (in the troope of learned poems of manye divine conceites) playeng the part of the poet *Codrus Meuius* and *Bauius* mentioned by *Iuuenall, Virgill,* and *Horace,* for which yet I dare not crave pardon (that falt being inexcusable) because it was in my choice whether I would vtter my follies or not; and then willinglie comitting a fault (for it is soe much a fault as it is voluntarilie donn) I cannot with reason craue patience or pardonn therof, wherfore ˙I must abide the censure [* leaf 2, back] and taxe of your lordships singuler Iudgement, although you maye Iustlie deale with me as *Silla* did with a badd poet, to whome writing an Epigram against *Scilla,* of boghed verses, some short and some longe, *Scylla* commanded a reward to be given to him, to thend he should never after compose anie more verses.

which yet, yf your Lordship should vse towards mee, I
would not (with Actius the poet) repent mee of these
my harshe rimes, because I maye hope hereafter to
wryte farr better; for your Lordship well knoweth
that our witts, inventions, and writings, are compared
to the frutes of trees which at their first encreasing are
hard, harshe and bitter, but in the end (by the comfort
of the beneficiall sonne) are made softe, swete, and ac-
ceptable to the pallate. But yf it should not fortune
mee hereafter to attayne a dellycate style, or more
wittie invention, to satisfie your Lordships expectance,
Yet I hope you will take these in good part, following
the example of *Lisander*, whoe did soe love and embrace
Poetrie (even of the worst sort) that he allwaies had the
badd Poet *Chyrill* with him in his warres, And with
silver fylled the Capp of *Antiochus* whoe had written but
[* leaf 3] homelie verses in his commendations: for which cause
I presume to consecrate to your Lordship the naked (for
soe I doe terme them, because they are not clothed with
engraven pictures) emblemes and Epigrams, what soever
they be, partlie drawen out of histories, and partlie out
of Phisicall Philosophie, but tending to moralitie, and
for the most part endinge in necessarie preceptes, and
perswatione to vertue. which I doubt not but your Lordshipp will accepte in such sorte as maye be answerable
to your honorable curtesey, and my desire, wherof the
firste is wont not to reiecte what before I haue offered
vnto you, and the other is readie to merit the continu-
ance of that which your Lordship hath before vouch-
safed vnto mee, soe that I cannot dispaire but that
your Lordship will take them in better parte then they
deserve. And that the rather, because some of them
are composed of thinges donn and sayed by such as
were well knowne to your Lordshipp, and to my self in
those yonger yeares when Lincolns Inn societie did
linke vs all in one cheyne of Amitie; and some of them

DEDICATION TO SIR THOMAS EGERTON.

are of other persons yet living, which of your Lordship are both loved & liked. But yf all these causes should not move your Lordship vnto their likinge, yet this good would growe vnto you by these follies, that they [* leaf 3, back] will give you cause of myrth, in notinge the lightnes and vayne conceites of the autor, which might have employed his endevours in more grave and beneficiall studies.

To discourse of the nature of Emblemes or Epigramms, what thinges be required to perfect them, and to what end they should be made, is nedeles to your Lordship, because *Paulus Iouius, Lucas Contiles, Cladius Minoes* vpon *Alciat*, & divers other menns labors intreating therof, are not vnknowen to you whose Iudgment and lerning hath peirced the depth of vniuersall knowledge; & therfore in vaine for mee to bring owles to *Athens*, or add water to the large Sea of your rare lerning, in superfluous itterating that wherof you are not Ignorant, beinge one whoe hath adorned your excellencie of lawe with bewtifull flowers of all [1]Philosophicall doctrine, as well divine as humane.

Thus, my good Lord, in all dutifull love commendinge these my slender poems (which may be equalled with Sir *Topas* ryme in *Chaucer*) vnto your good likinge, and comitting me to your honorable good favour and furtherance (to add oyle to the emptie lampe of my muse, for mayntenance of the light therof, which without the comfortable heate of your honorable patronage will soone be extinguished) I humblie take my leaue. from my howse in Clerkenwell Grene, the 20 of *December*[2] 1600.

Youre lordshippes in all dutye,
Francis Thynne
./·/ ·/·/·/·/

[1] *MS*. Pholosophicall
[2] The '20', 'December', and words after '1600', were filld in after the text was written, and in paler ink.

Embleames.

(1) Pietie and Impietie.

When false *Synon*, with tongue of guilefull tale,
had causd the monstrous woodden horse of *Greece*
to enter *Troy* wales, the bitter bale
of Priams state, flaminge in everie peece,   4
throughe raginge fiers, *Eneas*, full of pittie,
his sonne and father ledd forth of the Cittie.   6

He bare his aged Syre on shoulders stronge,—   7
oh sweete burdenn! the w*hi*ch the sonne did crave,—
and in his hand, Aschainus ledd alonge.
oh Fathers love! which never end maye haue.   10
his father, him self, his sonne, throughe *Grecian* foes
Eneas leades, when hee from *Troye* goes.   12

A lovinge deede of famous pietie,   13
when strength of youth releeveth feeble sprite;
a naturall deed of sonne his love and dutie,
to helpe his syre, w*hi*ch brought him into light;   16
for w*hi*ch this holie mann doth iustelie gaine
renowned fame, for ever to remayne.   18

But thow, oh wicked monster of beastlie minde,   19
Cruell and blodie *Nero*, the dregges of kinges,
contrarie to Nature, and fleshlie kinde,
(with greefe I doe abhorr to wright these thinges)   22
didst noe whit shame, thy mothers wombe to teare,
to see where shee did such a viper beare.   24

Wherfore to thee is left perpetuall shame, 25
to kill thy mother, to answere thy desire.
But to Eneas, doth growe eternall fame,
that sav'd his aged father from the fire : 28
hee, for reward, raisëd *Troy* walles againe ;
thow, for reward, in beastlie sort wert slaine. 30

(2) Vertue should not be condempned for one smale imperfection.

The heavenlie pallas of Celestiall skye,
resoundes with pleasant notes of musicks skill ;
the godds and goddesses, with mellodie,
to *Genius* doe sacrifice their fill. 4

They leave the Care they had for earthlie thinges ;
they daintie feastes freequent with sweet delight,
[leaf 5] before whose eyes faire *Venus* freshlie springes,
in apt measure daunsing, with comelie sight. 8

Shee footes it soe, with crowne of flowers in hand,
that all the godds extoll her for the same ;
but beinge prais'd by that moste sacred bande,
Momus beginns her daunsinge for to blame. 12

And findinge fault,—I knowe not well wherfore,
still redie, what best is, for to deface,—
affirmd the slipper which faire *Venus* wore,
with craaking noyse, her dauncinge did disgrace. 16

(3) Temperance abateth fleshlie Delightes.

Thow *Cithereane Venus*, I would knowe,
why thow, and *Cupid* houldinge of his bowe,

soe pensive bee, and over fier doe stande,
warming of thy feete, and warming of his hande?   4
Oh why? doth love and luste feele their decaye,
Yf *Ceres* and *Iacchus* be awaye?
Where Sobernes doth raigne amongst the wise,
there lust and hurtfull pleasures still doe frise.   8
They finde noe foode, nor anie warrs, can make   [leaf 5, back]
against the modest w*hi*ch sparing diet take.
but if that wealth and dronkennes beare stroke,
they, wicked warres of Lecherie, provoke.   12

(4) Death and Cupid.

The hatefull *Death* Ioynd to the *God of loue*
in one Cabine setled themselves to sleepe;
both had their bowes and shaftes, their might to prove;
the one gaue mirth, the other forct to weepe.   4
Thus blinded love, and death at this time blinde,
by chance doe meete, by chance doe harbor finde.   6

But starting forth of this their former rest,   7
heedlesse, the one, the others weapons caught:
the goulden shaftes from *Cupid, Death* berefte;
the dartes of *Death*, dame *Venus* sonne had raughte.   10
thus contrarie to kinde, and their nature,
Cupid doth slea, and *Death* doth love procure.   12

Ould doating fooles, more fit for *Carons shipp*,   13
that feele the goute, to grave w*hi*ch take their waye,
doe fall in love and youthfull-like doe skippe,
deckinge their heads with garlands fresh and gaye.   16
Their yeares and daies they easelie doe forgett,   [leaf 6]
and from their harte, colde sottishe sighes do fett.   18

But striplinges and yonge boyes that wounds receive
by yonge *Cupid*, then *Nestor*, yet more oulde,

against their kinde, their wished lift doe leave,
and vnto *Acheron* the waye doe houlde. 22
But *Cupid*, cease! and *Death*, thine owne stroke give!
Let yonge menn love, let ould menn cease to live. 24

(5) Art, the antidote against fortune.

On rolling ball doth fickle fortune stande;
on firme and setled square sitts *Mercurie*,
The god of Arts, with wisdomes rodd in hande:
wh*i*ch covertlie to vs doth signifie, 4
that fortunes power, vnconstant and still frayle,
against wisdome and art cannot prevaile. 6

ffor as the Sphere doth move continuallie, 7
and showes the course of fickle fortunes change,
soe doth the perfect square stand stedfastlie,
and never stirrs, though fortune liste to range. 10
[leaf 6, back] wherefore, Learne Artes, wh*i*ch allwaies stedfast prove;
therbye, hard happes of fortune to remove. 12

(6) Labour quencheth Lecherie.

Dictinian Diana, which
Of *Phœbus* borroweth lighte,
The glistring Queene of Woodes and groves,
and Ladie of the nighte, 4
Pursues the Hart—whose nimble feete
doe make him seeme to flie,—
with bowe and howndes, whose thundringe voice
doth Eccho in the Skye. 8
Yonge *Cupid* is not farr behinde,
but followeth on as as faste.
He shootes, but leaves no wound; in vaine
his fierie dartes are caste. 12

If Ignorant of cause thow bee,
why loue can take not holde
Of chast and travelinge Diane,
Of this thow maiste be bolde : 16
It is, for that shee not consumes
her golden time in vaine,
Nor Idle thoughts of wanton youth
doe harbor in her brayne ; 20
ffor, flienge Canker of slothfull eise, [leaf 7]
in huntinge spends the daye,
Wastinge her time with those delights,
to beate fond thoughts awaie. 24
Whoe therfore wiselie seekes to shunn
the force of *Cupids* Ire
vse exercise, flie Idle thoughtes ;
soe shalt thow quench his fire. 28

---

(7) Fortune.

There is a birde w*hi*ch takes the name
   of Paradise the faire,
Which allwaies lives, beatinge the winde,
   and flienge in the Ayre. 4
For envious nature him denies
   the helpe of resting feete,
wherby hee forced is, in th'ayre
   incessantlie to fleete. 8
Soe the vncertaine light and wilde
   fowle fortune variable,
whoe onlie in vnconstancie
   doth shewe herself most stable, 12
Doth never, in one pace or sorte, [leaf 7, back]
   prove constant in her power,
But doubtfull, fleeting here and there,
   still changing everie hower. 16

Wherefore the cunninge *Smirnians*
    her Image carved out,
With feete cut from her leggs, and sette
    on ball turninge aboute.   20
And for she could not setled stande,
    they sayd, as doth appeare,
'Sweet *Fortune*, thow dost flie in th'ayre,
    like birde depainted here.'   24

(8) Bryberie.

After his Fathers funerall,
    when as Tiberius went
Vnto his howse, his tender harte
    with pittie did relent;   4
For, seeinge of a wretched mann
    with scabbs and sores opprest,
On whom the suckinge flies did feed,
    not suffringe him to reste,   8
[leaf 8] Hee calld his servant, willinge him
    to drive awaye with speed,
Those Cormorantes which eate his fleshe,
    and forced him to bleede.   12
The mann obayed: but when he would
    haue beate those flies awaye,
Thee wretched sowle did him forbid,
    and mourninglie did saye: 16
"Yf that these gorged gnawinge flies,
    full glutted with my bloode,
Were beaten from their place of praye,
    newe troope, not half soe good,   20
Leane and greedie, with hungrie mawes,
    would then renewe my paine,
and suck my blood even to the death,
    not sparinge anie vayne.   24

Soe the old Iudge, once fullie fraughte
    with guiftes and briberie,
Will not be easilie ledd by guiftes
    to wrest the lawes awrye. 28
But hee that commeth newe in place,
    and thirsteth after gould,
Or his Iuditiall office buyes,
    with him there is noe hould; 32
for hee that buies, is forct to sell;   [leaf 8, back]
    and new corrupted Iudge
Takes all and more; and, for reward,
    is made a sinfull drudge. 36

---

(9) Immortallitie of the Sowle.

In former age, the *Ethnikes*, false gods servinge,
this solempne Ceremonie vsed to their dedd,
That when the paled corps went to buryenge,
a lawrell Crowne they wreathed about his head. 4

The cause wherof being asked by *Adrian*,
the famous Emperour of the *Romaine* state,
Byas replied: 'because that then, ech man
whome death reduceth to that happie state, 8

'forsaken hath all worldlie wretchednes;
they feele noe greefe, or sorrowes heavie payne;
wherfore, since they attaine such blessednes, 11
this garland shewes the Crowne which they doe gayne.'

Then since those vertuous *Ethnickes*, with such Ioye
addornd the funeralls of deceased wighte,
Whose faithelesse sowles, feirce *Pluto* did destroye,— [leaf 9]
for vnto them was shut the gate of lighte,— 16

Why should we faithfull *Christ*ians bewaile
our loved frendes, and celebrate with greefe—
the manne deceased, with scaping Satans gayle,
leaves woe, and winns a place of sweete releefe,— 20

Since vnto vs is made assured promise
for to enioye the vision of gods sight,
and to ascend celestiall place of blisse,
our god to praise, in whome wee shall delight. 24

(10) Sotted loue.

Autoritie and *Loue* will scarce agree,
and in one place are neuer found to bee;
for decencie must serve to ech estate,
and ech must live according to his fate. 4
Nice *Sardanapalus, th'assirian Kinge*,
a mann effeminate in losse livinge,
doth fall in love, and loves so foolishlie
that hee forgetts his state and maiestie. 8
[leaf 9, back] For, leaving of the kingdomes needfull charge,
and Heroike deedes, his kingdome to enlarge,
(oh sottishe loue !) hee whollie followeth luste;
hee followes Venus; in her doth hee truste; 12
hee locks himself from other companie;
and farr abasing his Regalitie,
not like a valiant mann, but all from kinde,
in woemens workes doth cheefest comfort finde: 16
hee cardes, and spinnes with distaffe in his hande;
hee workes and sowes, fast wrapt in *Venus* bande.
Wherfore yf thow wilt gayne an honest name,
and deedes performe to winn eternall fame, 20
Let Wemenn never soe bewitch thy witt,
as thow be forc'd from thine owne kinde to flitt.

(11) Pride.

The morrall *Seneca*, whose penn
intreatinge matters graue,
I finde, amongst his learned workes,
this worthie tale to haue:— 4

There was a kinge of highe renowne,
which iustice did vpholde.
to him, three sonns did nature give,
of courage feirce and bould. 8
To eche, the choice of birdes hee gaue, [leaf 10]
wherbye that hee might learne,
the severall humors of their minde
and manners to discerne. 12
The eldest, of his haughtie harte,
the Eagle prowd did chuse.
the second, of fiers disposition,
the hawke would not refuse. 16
The yongest, of a myleder minde,
the vulgar thrushe did take;
On whome the kinge bestowd his crowne,
and him his heire did make. 20
Iudge what the kinge ment by this guifte,
for I maye not disclose it.
And thow perhapps maie be deceived
in thikinge for to glose it. 24

---

(12) Patience.

The patient *Socrates*, true mirror of our life,
whoe for the godds did yeald his heavenlie breth,
twoe vnkinde wives did nourishe foolishlie,—
the first was blinde, the other had bleare eyes,— 4
of whome, good mann, he badlie was intreated.
Not once, nor twice, but allwaies when they raged, [leaf 10, back]
the one would beastlie spurne him like a dogg;
the other would belabour him with her fists; 8
all w*hi*ch hee bare with vertuous patience.
with bitter words, but being fiercelie baited,
hee was enforct to leave the vnquiet howse;
whoe, going forth, did rest him at the dore, 12

where long hee could not quiet sitt at ease,
but that these sprites, these furies fowle of hell,
did add more ill to former wickednes ;
for as hee satt with calme and gentle minde, 16
they on his hed did lothed vrine cast,
and shrewdlie wett him to the tender skinne.
But hee, w*hi*ch made of this a Iestinge sport,
as well aquainted with such brain sick witts, 20
vsed not revenge, but smilinglie did saye,
that after thunder, Rayne did still descende ;
for hee these wives did keepe, for to envre
his vertues rare, and patience to encrease. 24

---

(13) Liberalitie.

Why doe these virginns faire, the *Graces* three,
Ioues daughters, borne of *Eurinome* the brighte,
[leaf 11] On goddesse *Venus* waite in their degree,
Since they from seed of heaven did take there lighte ? 4
because from these the fruites of love proceed,
and loue is wonne by ech theire severall seed. 6

Their Rosiall faces, shap'd are after one, 7
as sister twinned, by reason ought to bee ;
the twoe, allwaies the third doe looke vpon ;
their youthfull age and bewtie doe agree : 10
Winged at feete they are ; they naked stande,
ech halsing other with their cristall hande. 12

The first wherof, *Aglaia* is named, 13
and worthie place doth hould amongst the reste :
A peerlesse Ladie, in ech place well famed,
shining in honnor deepe harbored in her breste. 16
the next, *Thalia*, w*hi*ch meaneth, as some teache,
faire flower of youth, and elloquence of speach. 18

The third, w*hi*ch wee call the faire *Ephrosine*, 19
to her sisters in vertue not behinde,

doth signifie (as learned menn define)
the pleasant mirth and frute of frendlie minde. 22
thus these *Charites*, these faire graces three,
the forme of love, and guiftes, presents to mee. 24

But why are they naked, without attyre? 25 [leaf 11, back]
because they showe the playnesse of the harte,
quite naked of decyte, and free from hire;
for in all guiftes, this Is the chefest parte, 28
that what we give, be donne with meere goodwill,
with simple and pure minde, devoid of ill. 30

Or ells because vnthankfull menn by kinde, 31
whoe naked are of curtesie and love,
Will naught bestowe, to shewe a gratefull minde;
besides all which, as wee continuallie prove, 34
the graces coffers are emptie and naked found;
for thankfull menn, with wealth cannot abound. 36

Whye are they virginns fayer, freshe, and bright? 37
for that therby wee covertlie are tould,
that of the frendlie guiftes receyvd, (by righte)
perpetuall memorie wee are bound to hould; 40
for, freshe in thankfull minde, wee must conceive
the deepe record of favours wee receive. 42

Why winged are their feete like mercurie? 43
because that, whoe doth guiftes or thanks impart,
must not deferr the same, but spedilie
performe the frute of his well willinge harte; 46 [leaf 12]
ffor hee gives twice, that quicklie and with speed
bestowes his guift to serve our present need. 48

Soe lovinglie, why are they Ioind in one? 49
ech one, in armes embracing of her mate;
and allwaies twoe, the third looking ypon?
It shewes, that frendes must live without debate, 52
that guiftes receyved, be paid with vsurie,
and that true frendes fayle not in miserie. 54

(14) Vertue of Herbes.

Whilste prudent *Epidaure*, the learned leeche,
the sacred herbes in fertill soyle doth seche,
with stedfast eye caste on the vallies deepe,
a tall yonge ladd,—w*hi*ch kepte the fearfull sheepe, 4
adorned with crowne of herbes faire, freshe, and greene,
of straunge devise, most orient to be seene,—
This *Epidaure* beheld in greate despite,
with *Basiliske* to vse most cruell fighte; 8
which poysoning beaste, this manne (with *Mars* his blowe)
did prostrate on the ground, and overthrowe.
Then *Epidaure* (iudginge some vertue rare
within the garland w*hi*ch the heardman ware,) 12
[leaf 12, back] Drewe nere, and by faire wordes did frendlie crave,
that hee, of him this herbie Crowne might haue.
wherto the herdman yealded his consent,
and then a freshe to basiliske hee went, 16
with that feirce beaste, movinge new fight againe,
in w*hi*ch the sillie mann was easelie slaine.
w*hi*ch donne, the phisition begann to saye,
'within this bowe, most secret vertue laye;' 20
and with this garland freshe, in everie Ioynt
the bodie of deade herdmann did annoynt.
forthwith the mann (a thinge to all menn straunge)
began to live, and life for deathe did change. 24
Such vertues doth the power of god divine,
for our releife, to yearthlie herbes assigne;
wherbye wee maie from menn diseases take,
Recover health, and dangers great forsake. 28

---

(15) Wine.

ffayne wouldst thow know wherfore the god
   last borne of Ioue his Thye,
Is winged on his hed, and whye
   swifte *Pegase* standeth bye. 4

And why the horse of true honnor [leaf 13]
    conioyned is to *Bacchus*,
The following verse, the springe and cause
    therof shall here discusse.   8
When people with *Amicla* did
    the grapes to *Bacchus* bringe,
She said, 'faire Bacchus, I see winges
    from out the hedd to springe;   12
Oh *Bacchus*, thow haste quivering winges,
    and heares that crowned bee
with greene Ivye; let *Gorgon horse*
    allwaies associate thee.   16
ffor *Bacchus* doth increase the blood,
    and force to vs it lendes;
To melancholie harts, both mirth
    and cooller freshe it sends.   20
It raiseth vpp dull mindes from Earth,
    to enterprise great thinges;
It comforteth the weake sinnowes,
    and strength to witt it bringes.   24
This doth the swifte *Pegasine* horse,
    conioynd with *Bacchus* tell,
But yet to vse wine moderatelie,
    for soe shall witt excell.'   28

---

(16) Mann. [leaf 13, back]

Behould, mann is the litle world,
    as *Gretiane* gaue him name,
And as the ould *Philosophers*
    did signifie the same.   4
ffor as the Sunn and Moone, bright lights,
    doe shine in azured *Skye*,
Soe hath the mann two sparkling eyes
    w*hi*ch vnder forehedd lie.   8

As goulden Sunn, with purple beames,
   in morning freshe doth springe,
And going vnder *Thetis* bedd,
   on world the shade doth bringe,   12
And soe doth rise and sett to vs,
   as other plannetts all,
Soe mann by byrth doth rise and springe,
   by death doth sett and fall.   16
The moving windes in skies that rowle,
   both hott and colde are founde;
and in the mouth of breathing mann,
   both colde and heate abound.   20
Our bones and members are the earth,
   the ayre in Lunges doth swell,
[leaf 14] The mouth and brayne doe water holde,
   the fire in hart doth dwell.   24
Thus mann is moyst, earthlie, and hott,
   with water, earth, and fire,
Be three the noblest Elements,
   which nature cann desire.   28
To infancie compared is
   the spring, sweet, freshe, and gaye;
the pleasant sommer vnto Youth,
   where strength and courage staie;   32
The ripenesse of manns firme estate
   doth fruitfull Autumne holde;
As crooked Age well likned is
   to winters frost and colde.   36

---

(17) Witt.

Nothing more smooth then artificiall glasse;
more brickle, yet there nothing maye be founde;
nothinge more white or fairer is on grounde
then congeald snowe, yet naught lesse firme can passe.   4
Soe, shining and fayre witts, in which abound

Invention, quick conceit, and answering,
three cheefest thinges, true praise deservinge,
haue their desert, and most doe run awrye,   8
Since finest white doth soonest take all staines,
and finest witts are ficklest of their braines,
whose self-conceit ruynes them vtterlie;
much like the Bees, whose honnie breedes their paines 12
by surfetting theron Immoderatelie,
for, from her sweete, coms her perplexitie.
Thus these rich witts, which fondlie deeme
    they all menn doe exceede,   16
By trusting to themselves too much,
    doe fayle themselves at neede.

(18) The subiect.

The statlie flower that faire rich *India* yeldes,   1
which goulden *Heliotropium* wee name,
the glorious *Marigolde* of fruitefull feildes,
the course of all his flowring time doth frame   4
after the light of *Phœbus* norishinge flame,
on which she waites with still attending eye,
windinge her self like sonne, circularlie.   7

Of which effect, the name she doth obtayne,   8
& *Heliotropium*, of sonne is calld.
ffor, when bright *Elios* with the fierie wayne,
his fower feirce steedes in purple morne hath stalld, 11
Then this strange flower (with Sable night appalld)
spredds forth her golden lockes, but hides her face
when *Phebus* bedds, as fearing some disgrace   14

Thus doth this noble flower, her homage due,   15
paie to her Lord whome shee doth imitate,
Houldinge that waie which her doth still pursue;
whose pliant minde, to vs doth intimate,   18
that as this flower, by natures hidden fate

doth followe still the turning course of Sunn,
wherin she pleasures till her life be donne,
So pliant subiects follow still,   22
    whilst rulinge Prince doth live,
The good or badd examples which
    his customd actions give.   25

---

(19) Diligence obtayneth Riches.

The simple Cock, that with a hungrie minde,   1
on sluttishe dunghill scrapte, in stedfast hope,
for his releefe, some feeding grayne to finde,
being forct to seeke within that litle scope   4
[leaf 13, back] to hym assigned by fortunes luckye lott,
a pretious Iewell for his paine hee gott;   6

which, though to him smale profitt it did give,   7
vnskillfull what the price therof mighte bee,
yet did it shewe the godds, for to releeve
the needie soule whome wee in labour see   10
turmoyle with swetting face, for to sustaine
his pore estate with such a luckie gaine.   12

---

(20) Vsurie.

The wealthie mann with blessings great indued,   1
raising his mightie halls to looke alofte,
whome never yet hath povertie pursued;
yf that his greedie minde be sett to ofte   4
to search for gaine, to fill his hungrie hart,
some froward chance the godds to him impart.   6

ffor a rich vsurer, which hordes of gould   7
entombed from some in armed chest dyd keepe,
not well content such heaped wealth to hould,
but vnderminding earth, did often creepe   10
in dungeons deepe, and mines of silver bright,
to rake for that which was his harts delight.   12

But Iust *Pluto*, a Iudge of rightfull rede, 13
when as this mann had entred goulden Cave,
his due desert, that was for him decreed,
as Iuste revenge permitted him to haue, 16
for hee by clodd (er hee might that auoyde)
of fallinge earth, was suddenlie destroyd. 18

Thus doe the godds to such as they enrich, 19
when thanklesse persons allwaies will appeare;
for thoughe to daye they send never soe mich,
yet when they please, they can with frowning cheere 22
spoyle them from all, but moste where they doe see
vnsaciate mindes still griping for to bee. 24

(21) Myrtilus Sheilde.

The famous souldier, *Myrtilus* the Knighte,
whose conquering minde did never stoope to feare,
in manye conflictes the Garland Palme did beare,
as well on Land, as in the Maryne fighte, 4
such was his force, such was his warrlike might,
still savinge his life by his helpfull Sheilde,
both in the swelling Sea and bloodie feilde.
On Land his faithfull sheild did him defend 8
from dobled strokes of stronge revenging foes;
and in mercilesse Seas devouringe woes,
this sheild, from drowninge, him to shoare did sende,
and brought him safe vnto his Iourneis ende: 12
in all mishapps, at everie time of neede,
this worthie Sheild did allwaies stand in steede.
  So, my good Lord, be you, I craue, to mee,
  Mirtilus sheild, where soe my bodie bee. 16

(22) Vayne Ostentations.

Wee dailie see the fruitfull *Phœbus* fier, 1
how richlie it brings forth the wished harvest,

which plenteouslie augments the owners hier,
one hundred foulde contentinge his request, 4
with his full eares still bending to the ground,
wherin greate store of grayne in tyme is found. 6
But bragg amongst the corne aspires proudlie, 7
on emptie eare lookinge aboue the reste,
advancinge his highe creste presumptuouslie
even to the starrs, as though he were the beste, 10
whoe, beinge lighte, and fruitlesse of all grayne,
for want of waight, showes all pride is vayne. 12

[leaf 17] Soe hee whome litle learninge doth commende, 13
is puft alofte with pride of highe conceite,
and deemes his witt maye with Minerve contende,
and scoole *Mercurie* with some queinte deceit; 16
but whoe that braggs, and deemes himself most learned,
most voide of art, by wise men is discernde;
Since he is allwaies somwhat, himself that nothinge
   deemes;
and he is nothinge found to be, himself that somwhat
   seemes. ——————— 20

(23) Losse of hurtfull thinges is gayne.

Producinge earth inrich'd, makes rich againe
the toylinge laborer hopinge fruitfull gayne;
but yf neglect, it vnmanurde growe,
corruptinge weedes and harmefull plants do flowe. 4
with wrootinge groyne, with feirce and warlike bore,
turnes vp and betters that bad lande before,
destroyeng those vnprofitable springes,
to frutefull land which such annoyance bringes, 8
which is not losse, but bettringe to the feilde,
more holsome frute then redie for to yeilde.
wherfore from thee, yf taken bee the thinge
which needlesse is, and doth not profitt bringe, 12

[leaf 17, back] nor losse nor greife, let that be vnto thee,
for weedes pluck'd vp, hurt not the ground, wee see.

(24) Internall vertues are best.

Sweet tasting aple, w*hi*ch this faire virginn beares,
In cristall hand doth shine with pleasinge hewe,
for in th'externall forme, to eye appeares
a glistring cullor which[1] doth delight renewe;   4   [1 *MS.* with]
but vnder that thinne Coate, fayre nature hides
more gratefull frute, w*hi*ch shee for mann provides.

Then thow, whome nature outwardlie hath graced
with comelie shape, externall forme to winne,   8
trust not therto; it wilbe soone defaced,
as of noe vse, like to the Aples skinn.
wherfore with vertue cloathe thy inwarde minde,
that th'outward shape therbye maye comfort fynde; 12
ffor what availes the gorgious showe
    of Apples outward skynn,
Yf the internall frute conteyne
    not pleasing taste therin?   16

---

(25) Threates of the inferior to be contemned. [leaf 18]

The melitane dogge, bredd onlie for delight,
whose force is smale, though voice be lowde and shrill,
with often barkinge putts greate doggs to flighte,
incensd with rage, as though he would them kill.   4

Yet thoughe hee threaten with moste cruell voice,
leppinge and runninge in haste for to devoure
the bloodie mastife, it lies not in his choice,
as wanting both a naturall strength and power.   8

ffor those greate dogges w*hi*ch flie not thence for feare,
contempne his threates, scorning revenge to seeke,
knowing the force and strength w*hi*ch they do beare
is overmuch for him w*hi*ch is so weake.   12

Soe hee whom strength and wisdome doth adorne,
the brawles and anger of the weake doth scorne,

since all the power wherin they doe abound,
consiste in wordes, which vanishe with the sound. 16

[leaf 18, back]

(26) Philosophie.

Ioues sonne, the valiant *Hercules*,
   whose worthye travayling peyne,
by his twelve labours, vnto him
   immortall fame did geyne,   4
made this the best and last labour,
   as glorie of them all,
That triple hedded *Cerberus*
   hee made to bee his thrall,   8
The mightie cheyned porter of
   The darke infernall hell,
where thinges obscure as dampned sprites
   in darke oblivion dwell.   12
which inwardlie to vs vnfoulds
   Philosophies triple kinde,
wherin doth rest the triple good
   of our celestiall minde.   16
ffor as three hedds of *Cerberus*
   doe from one boddie growe,
Soe from abstruse Philosophie,
   three severall springs doe flowe: 20
Divine, humane, and naturall,
   wherin consist the parts
[leaf 19] of heavenlie and terene creatures,
   and of all learned artes,   24
which are not conquered without
   great paynes of daye and night,
as *Hercules* by painfull toyle
   brought *Cerberus* to light,   28
That sharpe labour beinge the last,
   as cheefest and the best,
therin, all former labours of
   the bodie for to reste.   32

(27) Societie.

The purple Rose which first *Damasco* bredd,   1
adornd with cullor gratefull to the sight,
hath in it self a fragrant smells delight,
wherbye two sences of the mann is fedd.   4
thoughe other things to such faire shewe haue right,
yet maye they not equall this Rosie flower,
whose dayntie smell therin hath cheefest power.   7

Soe two faire dowries which mann doth enioye—   8
true perfecte love, and suer fidelitie—
firmelie preserve humane societie,   [leaf 19, back]
their frends assisting in ech hard annoye,   11
when want of ech brings noe securitie;
both which, this damaske rose doth well vnfoulde,
as honest hart, which fayth and love doth houlde.   14

ffor as the rose, depriv'd of pleasing smell,   15
retayning yet the cullor for the eye,
or havinge smell, wanting righte bewtie,
is not a rose, for both in that must dwell,   18
or ells it cannot other flowers defie,—
soe our societie, without love and fayth
is never perfect, as true reason sayth;
ffor where is perfect love, there trustie fayth is found,
and where assured trust doth dwell, there love must
    needs abound.   23

---

(28)
Counsell and vertue subdue deceipfull Persons.

The valiant knight whome *Perseus* wife did love,   1
whome she exilde for hee would not consent,
which tooke his name, as the effect doth prove,
of *Bellerus*, a prince to mischeife bent,   4
whose wicked deedes the *Corinthes* did susteyne
whilste over them his tyrannie did Raigne;—

[leaf 20] ffor when his *Heroike* hand had *Beller* slayne,
he called was *Bellepheron* the worthie, 8
whose chefest glorie and fame which he did gayne,
was, when he slue *Chimera* valiantlie,
The *Lician* monster, that people which destroyed,
and the Sea coastes on everie side annoyed. 12

ffor *Bellepheron,* this *Chimer* (as he fledd) 13
pursued on *Pegasus,* the horse of fame,
(which of *Medusas slater* first was bredd,
for vertuous deedes doe breed immortall fame), 16
and him, with force of minde and warlike hand
did slea, for naught maye strength and witt withstand.

Soe you, my Lord, borne vp on *Pegas* wynge, 19
doe fill the Earth and ayre with worthie prayse;
your rare exploytes, which of your vertue springes,
on *Fames* horse are spredd abroad allwaies, 22
since you haue slayne, by great advice and skill,
those *English Chimers* which this land did fill. 24

---

(29) Pleasures to be eschewed.

ffonde *Paris,* in vnbridled age doth chuse 1
the life which seldom sorteth to good ende;
[leaf 20, back] ffor in yonge yeares, whoe vertue doth refuse,
and doth on fading pleasures still attende, 4
can neither witt, nor wealth, nor honnor, gayne,
nor happie life in worldlie cares attayne. 6

He chose *Venus,* which 'madnes' is expounded, 7
and 'wanton life of pleasures' doth expresse;
he left *Pallas,* on which is rightlie grounded
the contemplation of all perfectnes; 10
he scorn'd *Iuno,* which 'wealth' doth signifie,
with thactive life meane that to multiplie.
  Then shonne delight, yf riches thow doe craue,
  Or perfect wisdome thow do seeke to haue. 14

(30) Vnitinge of Contraries make sound Iudgement.

Comforting *Ceres* Ioynd with hopps of bitter taste,
and faire waters, by art produce sweet liquors at the last,
not much inferior to *Bacchus* pleasant wyne,
as Emulus vnto that Ioyce which art doth well refine ; 4
for the sharpe taste of hopps, the water and the corne
doe mittigate, and make that sweet, which bitter was
    beforne :   6
which doth vs teach the waye, ech cause to handle well,
and howe in knotted difficults a Iudgement right to tell; [leaf 21]
for Ioyning contraries in peyse of equall weighte,   9
comparing the effects of both, the truth appeareth straite,
So adding hard to softe, and bitter to the sweete,
compounds a meane between them both, for Iudgment
    allwaies meet.   12

---

(31) Reuenge.

Dianiane dogge, with blinde furie inflamed,   1
fearinge the hurled stone which him offended,
with sharpe and threatning teeth whollie inraged,
doth bite the stone, on that to be revenged,   4
Iudginge noe other thinge but that dead stone,
of that his hurt, to bee the cause alone.   6

which fonde revenge doth others mirth provoke,   7
vnto himself much greatur hurte increasinge,
for guiltlesse stone cann never feele the stroke,
allthough the dogg cease not his cruell bitinge.   10
wherbye wee learne, not rashe reveng to take,
of that which of it self noe hurt doth make ;
ffor not the stone, but flinginge hande,
    the iust revenge doth crave,   14
and actors, not the instruments,
    due punishement should haue,

[leaf 21, back] Since to our selves more further paynes
    of greife wee shall procure,   18
yf rashe revenge, on guiltlesse cause,
    wee striue to put in vre.

(32) Peace.

Pluto, the god of worldlie wealth,
    which vnder yearth doth houlde
his goulden limittes and his bounds,
    with manie hills of goulde,   4
there governs at his cursed will,
    and goulden guiftes greate store,
with heaped Riches doth possesse
    a thowsand fould and more.   8
vnder whose feete, *Bellona* lies,
    still thirstinge after warrs,
a furious spoyler, and the cause
    of all tumultuous Iarrs.   12
But fayre sweet *Peace* doth lead *Pluto*,
    and draweth him with right hand,
And in lefte hand, *Amalthea*,
    the fruitfull horne, doth stande ;   16
ffor all thinges doe then flowe at large ;
    Bacchus and *Ceres* raigne ;
[leaf 22] Then *Halcyon* daies, then quiet rest,
    their triumphes doth retaine.   20
Then blodie *Mars*, cast to the grounde,
    to peace doth yeald his sword ;
but perfect peace descends from him
    Which was his fathers worde,   24
And first appeasd the Angrie god
    when hee, the loste mankinde
with peacefull concord, to our good,
    for evermore did bynde.   28

(33) Pouertie.

As fishe *Remora* staies the Shipp,
  which ells with prosperous wynde
Would sayle vnto the port of rest,
  sweete comfort for to finde,   4
Soe hated povertie, with greife
  of fortunes hard disgrace,
The Labors of the vertuous minde
  doth vtterlie deface: 8
ffor none soe noble vertue doth dwell in anie wight,
but want obscures it, forcing him to silence with dispight.

---

(34) Syluer worlde. [leaf 22, back]

The sacred Crowne adorning curled hayre,
and christall hand welding the kinglie mace,
the mounting Eagle which *Ganimede* did beare,
are ensignes of the mightie Ioue his grace.   4
All which doe shewe the sylver world fore past,
when Cuntrey Swayne prepared the happie soyle,
and with his seede the Earth did overcaste,
which yoked oxe did teare vp with his toyle.   8
Before which tyme the fertyle earth gaue out
her blessed frute, thoughe she vntilled laye,
And *Saturne* grave, the world did rule about,
the goulden age which did to vs bewraye;   12
But when that *Ioue* begann his Silver raigne,
and had expelde his father from his lande,
the feildes were tylld with greate & sweating payne,
and Wearied Oxe and horse, did mourning stand.   16

---

(35) Enuye.

The mightie *Ioue* from highest heaven did sende   1
the fayer *Phœbus*, these gratefull newes to tell

to wicked virginns, in vice which did excell,
this greate favour that hee to them would lende, 4
[leaf 23] That for herself, what anie one did crave
of him, her fellowe, duble that should haue. 6

fforthwith, the monster vilde of all mankinde, 7
w*hi*ch gnawes her harte, and teares our worthie fame,
stepte forth and said, '*Apollo*, graunt this same,
that I one eye maye loose! for soe I finde 10
my fellowe shall loose her twoe eyes and sight.'
all w*hi*ch she spake through envie and despight. 12

Thus fretting envie, Ioyeng in our payne, 13
pininge her self when good to vs doth growe,
and fatting fast when hurte or losse doth flowe,
in all mischeif findinge her chefest gayne, 16
of her own hurte, nothing doth force at all,
yf double that vnto her neighbour fall. 18

---

(36) Our terme or limit of life not remoueable.

ffrom neck it hath the humane shape,
   the rest a piller stone :
Thus *Terminus* the god is made,
   of all the godds alone ; 4
[leaf 23, back] Whome, when the ruler of the starrs
   beheld with scornefull face,
Hee willd him to depart the feilde,
   and leaue to him the place. 8
But *Terminus*, all confident,
   did bouldlie to him saye,
'I yeald to none': the septred Ioue
   could not drive him awaye. 12
Hee standeth fixte, not to be moved,
   whome wee cannot intreate
with price, nor prayer, with wordes, nor giftes,
   nor yet with angrie threate. 16

Soe are the fixed bonds w*hi*ch god
    doth limit to our daies,
not to be changed or removed,
    to lengthe them anie waies.   20

(37) God slowlie punisheth.

What doth the waightie millstone meane,
    not turned by the wynde?
Of heavenly god it signifies
    the nature and the kynde.   4
The father of celestiall sprit*es*,   [leaf 24]
    of mortall menn the Kinge,
His thunder bolts doth rarelie shoote,
    or lightnings downe doth flinge.   8
With slowe and stealinge pace, the wrath
    of god doth on vs fall,
As one w*hi*ch gentlie doth expect
    that wee for mercye call.   12
But when continnued patience
    doth breake his former bande,
His anger is to furie turnd,
    he strikes with heavie hande;   16
and with iust doblinge of the payne,
    the grevous punishment
doth recompence the long delaye,
    vnlesse wee doe repent.   20
ffor as millstone, once forct to turne
    by rage of boystrous winde,
without regard, eche subiect thinge
    doth into powder grynde,—   24
Soe clemencie of god, once broke
    by our continuall sinne,
Doth vs torment with greater yre,
    our sowles therbye to winne.   28

(38) Dull witts.

The cheife of gods, the mightie *Ioue*,
   conceived in his brayne,
And in newe sort did beare a childe,
   yf Poets trulye fayne.   4

But when that wonderfull burthen,
   to worlde he could not leaue,
The fierie god, the lame *Vulcan*,
   with Axe his hed did cleaue.   8

Then Armed *Pallas* lepped forth,
   true wisdome by her kinde,
for not of fleshe doth wisdome growe,
   but of the precious minde;   12

ffor triple power of heavenlie minde,
   which in the brayne doth dwell,
doth make vs like the triple god,
   in wisdome to excell.   16

Some kinde of men there are, whose witt
   soe pore wee often see,
As, but with payne and longe dayes toyle,
   naughte will engendered bee;   20

ffrom whome their wisdome must be drawen
   (since they want learned speeche)
As *Pallas* was from *Ioue* his hedd,
   as doth this Embleme teache.   24

---

(39) The wretched not to be Doblie greiued.

The birde of *Ioue*, the Eagle of flight most free,   1
   with manye bites, the naked hart doth teare,
of wretch *Prometheus*, hanging on the tree,
   which for our skill doth this good lesson beare: 4
In this sorte not to vexe with doble greefe
A wretched mann deprived of releefe,   6

But rather showld, with words of myledest kinde, 7
    a plaister give, to cure his greevous wound;
for to the same, sweet pittie doth vs bynde,
    Since in godds nature dailie that is found, 10
and his preeceptes, in tables graven in stone,
gives vs in charge, the wretched to be none. 12

ffor hee whose tender hart with pittie dighte 13
    vnto the sicke doth reache his helpinge ayde,
and partner of the waight of burdened wighte
    doth ease his payne when hee is overlayed, 16
Amongst the heavenlie Saints shall firmelie gayne   [leaf 25, back]
A memorable name, still to remayne. 18

---

(40) Noe impuritie in heauen.

The blinded boye, which with his peircinge darts 1
and tender stroke, the heavenlie godds did wound,
felt greate delight to scorche their pliant harts,
since fellowe like amongst them he was found; 4
but when both sexes of gods did feele such blowe,
oft times greate warrs amongst themselvs did growe. 6

Then prudent *Ioue*, seinge that fyerie broyle 7
to rise by weapons which *Cupido* bare,
fearinge the godds would one annother spoyle,
the bowes and shaftes from *Cupids* backe he tare; 10
and with greate reason, for that boyes disgrace,
did throwe him downe from out that sacred place; 12

ffor the first father which hath made the skye 13
must keepe the heavenlie feilds most cleane & pure;
Soe *Lucifer*, the prowde, clyming on hye,
was caste from heaven, in hell for to indure; 16
for naught vncleane, as sacred letters tell,
in this most holie Cittie once may dwell. 18

(41) Honor and rewarde nourisheth artes.

[leaf 26]

Shewe mee, sweete muse, why thow and all the rest
w*h*ich heavenlie spheres doe guide with harmonie,
were fostred vp with milke from Christall brest
of *Euphemen* distillinge plenteouslie.   4

Our nurce, her name doth well the same vnfold,
yf wiselie thow the sence therof dost knowe,
for *Euphemen*, none other thinge doth hould,
but this w*h*ich from that greekishe man doth flowe.   8

Since *Euphemen* doth onelie signifie
good fame, good name, a good report & prayse,
true honour, due reward, and perfect glorie,
w*h*ich nourishe Artes, and learned men allwaies.   12
    ffor without that, who, learning would applie,
    or weare himself with paine & miserie?   14

---

(42) Eloquence.

Some Learned menn affirme by abstruce skill   1
that *Proteus*, god and author of eche thinge,

[leaf 26, back] who into severall formes, at his owne will,
oft turnd him self, as did occasion springe,   4
    exprest a man, w*h*ich fullie could expounde
    ech severall thinge w*h*ich was in nature founde.   6

Some sayed he was a man of pretious witt,   7
and greatlie skilld in kinglie government;
for they w*h*ich at the Helme of state doth sitt,
must see wherto their subiects most are bent,   10
and turne him self into eche severall minde,
yf calmed realme he wishe, or hope to finde.   12

But I this *Proteus* severall formes doe deeme,   13
the force of Eloquence for to vnfould;
for as he oft did make his shape to seeme
a beast, a fowle, greene earth, or water cowlde,   16

Soe devyne Eloquence, mens mindes doth change,
Even as it lists, to like of thinges most straunge. 18

(43) Art cannot take awaye the vice of nature.

The healthfull bathe w*hi*ch daielie wee doe see
to cure the sores and fleshe of lothsome skinn,
cann never make the Negro white to bee,
or clense the harlot from her loathed sinne, 4
ffor such defaults as nature dothe committ [leaf 27]
in the outward shape w*hi*ch she doth vs impart,
or such defaults as growe by minde or witt
cannot be cured by anie outward art; 8
    ffor though a time wee bridle natures strength,
    She will break forth, and houlde her course at length.

(44) Fortune.

As goulden Sonne doth worke from out the Skye
divers effectes, and those exceedinge straunge,
Soe wandringe fortune, by incertaintie,
workes her effectes with sundrie kindes of change. 4

ffor somm she doth oppresse with miserie,
ffrom dunghill, raysinge some to heapes of gould
Some she castes downe from great nobilitie,
and makes a clowne a noble place to hould. 8

Shee gives Kingdomes, shee takes them backe againe,
her wheele still turnes, not havinge anie staye;
she subvertes all, even as she please to fayne;
and as with ball, soe with the world doth playe. 12
    In honnors Chaire, then see that thow sitt faste,
    Least with her checke shee mate thee at the laste. 14

(45) Ganymede.

[leaf 27, back]
Yea, impure mindes whom vncleane lusts defile   1
against the rightfull course of natures kinde,
which perverslie your pleasant witts beguile,
with Ioue his loue, which Ganymede did finde,   4
deme that sweet fayre which forct the godds to love,
was sacred, and noe common lust did prove.   6

which Ganimede his name doth well expresse;   7
for that, a prudent mann, doth signifie,
who doth his minde to Heavenlie things addresse,
and flies to Heaven by livinge vertuouslie,   10
then which, on earth, nought cann be fairer founde,
causinge goddes love to vs for to abounde.   12

    Then with true wisdome see
        godds favour thow deserve,
    In goulden cupp, with heavenlie drinke
        of Nectar, him to serve.   16

(46) Eloquent wisdome.

The talking byrd, which gloriously is cladd   1
By natures guise in robe of *Emeraud* greene,
[leaf 28] And *Tyryan* feathers gorgious to be seene,
with humane tongue and voice which art doth add,   4
of eloquent mann the worthie Tipe is hadd,
Such one as Tullie sayes he never found,
thoughe in sweet speech learn'd oratours abounde.   7

The Sea *Tortoys*, his howse which beares on back,   8
foure footed, shell clothed, and of fearefull sounde,
short hedded, Snake necked, without bowells fownde,
of hideous sight, and which warm blood doth lack,   11
whose Armor naught can peirce, of pase most slack,
true wisdomes signe doth vnto vs present,
And stayed minde to perfect wisdome bent.   14

Our Parrot then, vpon this Tortoys plac'de,   15
to vs doth note, by *Egiptian* misterie,
the sound effect of wisdomes veritie,
with *Mercuries* flowing tongue most swetelie grac'd, 18
which Ioynd in one, can never be defac'd;
wherof a truer mirror none maye knowe
then you, in whome such famous guiftes doe flowe : 21
Then live in hapie health,
    since *Mercuries* worthie Arte,
And learn'd *Mineruas* skill,
    doth harbour in your harte.   25

---

(47) Poetrye. [leaf 28, back]

The artificiall Scale composd of gould,
the shyning mettall to *Phebus* consecrate,
doth fayre imprint the figure he doth hould
in plyant waxe, to secrecie dedicate ;   4
that wax, transforming to his forme aright,
a gladsome pleasure to a Curious sight.   6

And golden Poet fedd with *Appollos* muse,   7
by his *Emphatick* verse of heavenlie kinde,
such charming power in reader doth infuse,
and grave such passions in his pliant mynde,   10
that he is metamorphos'd with delight
into the autors secret thoughts and sprighte ;   12
ffor why, such enargye and life
    doth in learn'd verse abound,
That sence, and witt, and hart, it doth
    both ravishe and confounde.   16

---

(48) Ensignes of the Clergye.

Thow doest demaund of me,
    why this right hand doth houlde

     the slipperie Ele, w*hi*ch turnes himself
      in circle manifoulde;   4
[leaf 29] And whye the guelye arme
      in midst of Sheild is placed,
     Of Asured cullour, whose bright shine
      the firmament hath graced.   8
     The blewishe Scuttchion doth present
      the vawted Skye,
     Deenotinge that the spirituall man
      should love the things on hye.   12
     The reddishe cullor doth declare
      the modest shame
     which in his countenance should dwell,
      a vertuous life to frame.   16
     The Ele prest with the hand,
      doth teach him to refrayne
     His lipps and tongue from vttring wordes
      deceiptfull, false, or vayne.   20
     This must the learned Clarke
      allwaies record in mynde,
     yf of Saluation, care he haue,
      or comfort hope to finde;   24
     ffor as the slipprye Ele
      not prest, doth slide awaye,
     So doth the slipprye tongue, the thoughts
      of inward minde bewraye.   28
[leaf 29, back] The white cullor of Ele
      declares that all his deedes
     Should be white, pure, and Innocent,
      w*hi*ch from his hart proceedes. 32
     Thus yf he frame his life,
      imbraced still is hee
     Of godd and of the world, to w*hi*ch
      he shall example bee.   36

(49) Flatterers.

There is a kinde of men, whome hell hath bredd,
Deceit hath nourc'd, and doble speech hath fedd;
naked of vertue, and impudent of face,
abhord of all, exilde from everie place,   4
ffalse flatterers nam'd, themselves wh*i*ch change
to every fashion, though never soe strange.
These doth the fishe *Polipus* represent,
in his conditions wh*i*ch be impudent,   8
Turning his cullor to everie kinde of Hue,
of everie obiect offerd to his viewe,
wherbye he maye, with bayt of cloked change,
deceyve the fishe wh*i*ch in the deepe do range,   12
Therbye more lightlie for to winn his praye,   [leaf 30]
to gorge his gluttenous mawe with foode allwaye.
Soe the false Parisites themselves doe wynde
to divers formes, as tyme and place they fynde,   16
Changinge themselves to ech mans severall vayne,
foode, wealth, or clothinge, therbye to attayne,
Deceyvinge such as in them put their trust,
paynelesse to serve their Hungrye mawe & lust,   20
and without labour to releeve their need,
worse then the Crowes on carrion wh*i*ch doe feed,
for they, dead bodies onlie doe devoure,
when these, the livinge doe consume ech hower.   24

---

(50) Our betters or enemies not to be prouoked with wordes.

Strymonian Cranes, wh*i*ch by their ayerie flight
preserv'd the wise *Deucalion* from the flood,
are taught by natures beneficiall lighte
to seek helping art for their better good;   4
for wh*i*ch, when they crosse frozen *Taurus* hill,
ech one, a stone doth carrie in his bill,

wherby they stopp the lowde voice of their crye,
leaste when they passe that huge and ragged mounteyne,
[leaf 30, back] The Queene of birdes, their foe, should them discrie, 9
and their voyce make them praye to Ioue his swayne;
but having overgone that dangerous place,
they leave those stones, and forth direct their pace. 12

Soe men, whome art and nature doth adorne,
should silent be, for feare of followinge hate,
and not with wordes, their betters for to scorne,
or ells their foes by tongue to Irritate. 16
for gentle speech, or silence, at the length
doth swage or keepe vs from our Ennemies strength,
    which over pas'd, wee maie with courage bould
    keepe on the course of life wee meane to hould. 20

---

(51) Wisdome and Strength are to be Ioyned.

Doe tell, rude verse, why that pure virginn fayre,
borne of *Ioues* brayne by helpe of *Vulcans* skill,
came armed forth into the Shining ayre,
not borne of Humane fleshe by natures will, 4
but whole begott of heavenlie seede and light,
being *Pallas* and *Minerua* call'd by right. 6
[leaf 31] It shewes that wisdome doth from good discend, 7
not borne of fleshe, nor bredd of Earthlie kinde.
that shee came armed forth, it doth pretende
that wisdome without strength is but a wynde; 10
and strength without wisdome, subversion brings,
but Ioyn'd in one, doe conquer hardest thinges. 12

---

(52) The meane.

The *Daulian Philomell*, whose warblinge voice 1
descants the musick of natures sweete delight,
in her self notes soe greatlie doth reioyce,
that with the same she putts her life to flight, 4

soe swetelie yealdes this nightingale her sprite;
And vegitive plantes, watered with the meane,
doe springe; but overmuch, doe wither cleane. 7

Soe the excesse in everie Earthlie thinge, 8
and the extreame in everie fadinge kinde,
vncured hurt vnto it self doth bringe,
and extreame greife vnloked for doth finde; 11
ffor learned *Flaccus* putts vs still in minde
that witt is follie, and right iniustice named,
and vertue vice, beyond the meane once framed. 14

---

(53) Not to climbe ouer highe. [leaf 31, back]

Bellerephon, which ruld without offence,
whome fretting envie could not make to yealde,
nor *Pretus* wife to incest could incense,
nor triple monster force to flie the feilde, 4

Did once ascend to his immortall fame,
the horse of honnor stabled in the skye;
but not of power, that vntam'd beaste to tame,
hedlonge is throwne to ground most worthilie. 8

Then thow which doste highe dignities attayne,
and clothed art with honnors purple gowne,
aspire not higher, least to thy bitter payne,
with extreame shame thow hedlonge tumble downe, 12
By fall, pervertinge former good
    for which thow hast byn praysed,
And blemishing those worthie partes
    which thee to honnor raysed. 16

---

(54) Monument of a harlott.

Whose tombe is this? whose bones doth this contayne?
the *Ephereian Lais* here doth lie,
whose peerelesse bewtie, wanton *Greece* did stayne [leaf 32]
with her highe prys'd excessive Lecherie; 4

but wo, alas! sham'd not their destinie
to cut her fatall thred which was soe faire,
to whome to *Corinth* all men did repayre. 7

No, she was with crooked age foreworne, 8
her frowinced face her bewtie had defac'd,
And like a woman which weare all forlorne,
and that of *Venus* nowe noe more was grac'd, 11
her christall glasse on *Venus* wall she placed,
as lothinge in that mirror for to prye,
her wrinkled eyes and cheekes for to espie. 14

Vppon whose curious tombe, engraven by skill, 15
did stand a feirce and cruell Lyonesse,
which did the simple Ram, even at her will,
hould by the Loynes with clawes of bludinesse; 18
which vnto vs this morrall did expresse,
that by the Loynes she still did hould and keepe
her fonde lovers, as Lyonesse doth the Sheepe. 21

(55) Earthlie mindes.

The statelie Stagg, whose hornes threaten the skye, 1
is sencelesse dombe, not hearinge anie sounde
of hungrie dogges that seekes him eagerlie,
or hunters voice which doth in woodes rebounde, 4
whilst hee with grynding teeth feedes on the ground,
except he first his hed from Earth erect,
wherby the hearinge sence maye them detect. 7

Soe mortall men, full fraught with worldlie toyes, 8
whose earthlie mynde, howsd in such brutish wight,
(beastlie feeding on fleshlie fadinge Ioyes,)
cannot conceive the words of heavenlie spright, 11
nor heare the gladsome voice of heavens delight,
Leaste to the skye his hanging hed he raise,
from earth of Sinn, and sowles corrupting waies. 14

(56) The olde Testament.

The Oke, bearing a corne, *Ioues* sacred tree,
which, to wise *Greekes*, the *Oracles* did lend;
the Ayerye spredding beech, whose arms wee see,
frise clothed frut vnto the world doth sende;   4
In former Ages, and Earths infancie,
when eche Creature to natures lawe did bend,
with their swete nourishing mast fedd plenteouslie
our Aunciēt Syres, of other food depriued;   8
But wee, through Goddesse *Ceres* helpe reviued,
comforting corne for Sustenance obteyne,
A pleasant foode, more exellent by kinde.
Soe nowe these trees noe needfull vse doe gayne,   12
but that to shade and buildinges they are sign'd,
which Moses lawe to vs doth signifie,
that was but mast, as stifneckd Iewes maye finde,
and shaddowes of the followinge veritie;   16
for nowe the immortall sonne of deitie,
Our *Sauiour Christ*, the autor of all good,
with rare bountie doth give abundantlie
his heavenlie corne to bee our dailie food;   20
wherbye wee leaue that mast and Iewish meate,
and hould that elder lawe confirm'd by blood
of beastes, and which but shaddowes doth repeate,
as figures onelie of Christes healthfull lore,   24
which is the perfect meate, whose signe the Iewes did
    eate before.

---

(57) Sophistrie.

Saturns daughter, and *Ioue* his Iealious wife,
Queene of Riches, pleasure of this life,
the angrie *Iuno* by her queint device,
self louing *Syrens* falslye did intyce   4
in songe with the sweete muses to contend.
these *Syrens* were, as autors doe pretend,

faire virgings, which in squamous fishe did end,
and fishe with virgins faces forth did send :   8
Wemen lacking natures feete of righte,
and fethered fowles wanting winges for flight,
which, though nature denye soe to combyne,
yet were they such as wee do here defyne,   12
conteyned in the holie number three,
whose names, significant are knowen to bee :
Parthenos virginn, with sweete *Ligia*,
and the most daintie white *Leucosia*,   16
who doth in false bewitching tunes excell,
wherby they sacred muses did compell
with them to singe, victorious crowne to gayne ;
which learned muses did at first disdayne,   20
all though at length they yealded full consent,
and to their witlesse challeng did relent ;
[leaf 34] when with their shrill and most celestiall sound,
those prowde *Syrens* they easilie did confound,   24
by iustice lawe ; for whoe maye well compare
the muses musick naturall and rare,
to the deceitfull Captious *Syrens* skill,
with which they all lascivious eares doe fill ?   28
The muses then, full victors in the feilde,
vnplum'd those Syrens whome they forct to yeald,
and from them all their glorious fethers take,
wherof triumphant crownes they dulie make ;   32
which *mithologians* thus doe moralize :
the muses, note the doctrine of the wise,
and perfect wisdome, which victoriouslie
triumphes on crag'd deceitfull Sophistrie,   36
which by false *Syrens* we doe signifie.
for what ells doe their fethers notifie,
but foolishe words, wanting true reasons ground,
which light, like fethers toste in wynde, are founde ? 40
these doth true wisdome overthrowe in Scorne,
and with faire crowne therof, her hedd adorne.

(58) Ingratitude.

The stam'ringe Cuckooe, whose lewd voice doth greeve 1
the daintie eares with her fowle note dismay'd,
In the *Currucas* neste doth her releeve, [leaf 34, back]
Suckinge the Egges w*h*ich that heysuge hath laid; 4
in lue wherof, her owne egg she doth leave,
wherbye she doth the gentle bird deceyve. 6

W*h*ich that simple heysuge findinge in place 7
(pore sillie foole, not knowinge of this guile),
doth lovinglie nourishe with moothers grace,
hatchinge those Egges that did her bed defile, 10
by dailie food them fostring, as they were
of her owne kinde, and her true forme did beare. 12

But these vile bastards, as they growe in strength, 13
and fethered are with winges of trecherie,
their nource and moother doe assault at length,
with thankles mouth tearing her cruellie, 16
till peecemeale they devoure ech severall part,
and suck the blood of their dames loving hart. 18

Soe, wicked menn, the bastards of mankinde, 19
whome neither love nor reasonn cann alure,
whome others great rewards, to them should bynde,
because their life is nourished by their cure, 22
Acteons curres, and thanklesse menn doe prove,
wounding their patrons whome they ought to loue. 24

---

(59) Children in youth to be framed. [leaf 35]

In yongest yeares, when will and strength doe want, 1
doe frame the child like to the growinge plant,
w*h*ich yonge and tender thow maist wrye and bende
vnto what forme thy fancie shall intende; 4
but once a tree, and growen to height of strength,
noe force cann make him bowe or bend at length. 6

(60) Of the same.

As tender whelpe, whome natures skill hath taught 1
by her instinct to hunt and chuse the game,
to his perfection never yet is broughte,
nor for to doe his maisters will can frame, 4
till first his tutor, crosse his necke doe tye
a litle bat, to frame his whelpe therbye. 6

ffor that Invres and teacheth him, to beare 7
the Yoke in youth, which age would not Indure,
and doth compell him to obedient feare,
which in his age he never should procure. 10
in youth then, hange about the child his neck
the staffe of feare, his stubbornes to check ;
Soe he shall learne, in age for to obaye,
[leaf 35, back] In youth that first was taught the readie waye. 14

(61) Benefitts.

The silver Moone, *Diana* Virgine bright,
on mortall creatours powred her moystening light,
wherwith she doth adorne the Sable nighte,
whose sleepinge mantle dimms the peircinge sight ; 4
which gladsome shine she takes abundantlie
from her beloved spowse, who favourablie
doth spredd his goulden beames most liberallie
on that faire *Phebee* full of curtesie. 8
Thus, like the liberall moone, wee should bestowe
the bennefitts which from highe *Ioue* doe flowe
vnto vs mortall creatures here belowe,
vpon our neighbours, whome wee needie knowe, 12
ffor soe the beneficiall heavens
    doe teach vs by their kynde,
whose comfortable vertues, wee
    doe by their influence finde. 16

(62) Prodigalitie.

The craftie ffox, with longe and bushye tayle, 1
doth allwaies clense and sweepe the durtie soyle,
wherat the mockinge Ape begann to Rayle,
for that his heavie tayle was clogging toyle 4
and in his chase did put him oft to foyle,
when he was quick, and nimblie, clym'd ech tree,
as being taylesse, lighter for to bee. 7

But scoffers must rescoffed be againe; 8
for subtile fox, with answer soone replied,
and rightlie said it was noe heavie payne
to beare those thinges which nature did provide, 11
our open shame, and fowle mishapes, to hyde;
for better was, to cover secretlie
the hinder partes, then shewe them lothsomlie. 14

Thus did the foxe the truer cause defende, 15
since much better are superfluities
which vs adorne, and profitt doe pretende,
then want of things to hide deformities. 18
So prodigall men, with their extremities,
ffarr better are in spending lavishlie,
then he that wants to serve necessitie. 21
And witlesse vnthriftes, which
   superfluouslie do spende,
Doe much more good then such
   as hordinge do attende. 25

---

(63) To m^r Thomas Valence.

My Valence, to thy learned vewe
   this skillesse vers I sende,
the fruit of my well wishing hart,
   and guifte of faythfull frende; 4
doe take it with like lovinge minde,
   to aunswer my desart,

whome frowninge fortune hath denied
    a better to imparte.   8
The frutefull bough of sacred Olive,
    the braunch of peacefull tree,
the leaves of oylie healthful frute
    that allwaies greene wilbe;   12
Which never lose their naturall shewe,
    whose leaves doe never fall,
ffor which the *Romans* in lesse triumphes
    were crowned therwithall,   16
[leaf 37] As were the troopes of valiant knightes,
    because this holie tree,
To warlike *Pallas* consecrate
    ys allwaies found to bee;   20
vpon which sacred florishinge bough
    I offer to thine eyes
A gentle Swarme of Wittie Bees
    and honnie bearinge flies,   24
By which, as former learned menn
    did vnto vs present,
Prosperitie of dailie health,
    and minde to quiet bent;   28
So by the same I wishe to thee
    like health and quiet minde,
with good successe, wherby thow mayest
    perpetuall comfort finde;   32
Like Olive never to decaye,
    but allwaies freshe to springe,
In peace of minde, in peace of tyme,
    Eternall peace to bringe;   36
ffor yf we warr within our selves,
    distract with everie thought,
Desired health doth still decaye,
    Sicknes is dailie wrought.   40
[leaf 37, back] Then to this peace and quiet rest
    is Ioyn'd sweete nutriment,

ffor whoe delights in bitter foode,
 to shorter life is bent;   44
ffor that our Auncient fathers ment,
 by addinge to this tree
Dedalan bees, bright *Phebus* babes,
 which good phisitions bee.   48
Since from the Olive, oyle distills,
 the Bees sweet honie give,
both w*h*ich, the weake and feble parts
 with comfort do releeve.   52
'And who, longe life,' saies *Democrite*,
 'would winne for payne and toyle,
must moyst his inward parts w*i*th honnie,
 and outward parts with oyle.'   56
So shall continuall prosperous health,
 longe life for vs obtayne,
wh*i*ch as before, soe nowe to thee,
 I freindlie wishe againe.   60

---

(64) Strangers more freindlie to vs then our owne kinde and kindred. [leaf 38]

My loved frend, and lovinge therwithall, 1
the same even nowe w*h*ich former tymes did finde,
against true freindshipps bande, howe maye it fall
that I should shewe my self soe farr vnkinde, 4
as to lett slipp our frendship out of minde?
wherfore this Embleme, wh*i*ch I frendlie ment,
take with like love as I the same present. 7

The pretie youth, *Telemachus* the fayre, 8
the pledge most deere to *Vlisses* eloquent,
and chaste *Penelope*, which with despaire
did feed her hungrie sutors hote intent, 11
and never would to theire desire relent,
did fall from crooked shore, sitting at ease,
into the raveninge wombe of raging Seas. 14

fforthwith, full fraught with love and pietie, 15
the *Arionian Dolphins* were at hand,
whose gentle barks receyv'd him lovinglie,
and from the deepe restored him to land, 18
Savinge his life; wherbye wee vnderstand,
That straungers to our kinde and to our bloode,
then our owne kinde and kinn, do vs more good,

[leaf 38, back] And that th' vntamed Seas 22
    breed fishe of better kinde,
Then pleasant Earth doth yealde
    vs menn of lovinge minde. 25

[*Leaf* 39 *is blank, both sides.*]

[Epigrams.]

Epigramms. [leaf 40]

(1) The Armes of England.

The sacred Lyon of *Iudeas* princelie lyne, 1
which weldes the scepter of the glorious skye,
of *Iesses* roote the flowers most divine,
whose heavenlie smell feedes our mortallitie, 4
protect (moste worthie Queene) from all annoye
Thy Realme, thy Lyons, and thy flowers of Ioye. 6

(2) Crisopeia.

My dolefull muse, bewayle in mournefull rimes, 1
with sighinge penn, with Inke of deepe lament,
the bitter galls of our vnhappie times,
and pore estate of those to vertue bent; 4
for he whome vertue hath to honnor raised,
treades downe all those which are for vertue praised. 6

O Sea of sorrowe! wherin wee sayle with greife, 7
O gulfe of greife! wherin wee drowne with payne,
since vertue cannot finde her due releeife,
but to faire *Crisopeia* shee retayne, 10
whoe sotts him soe with her bewitchinge sight, [leaf 40, back]
that but she speake, vertue doth loose her right. 12

Ye noble mindes, reiect your worthie partes, 13
let valour sleepe, your Heroike deedes will fayle;
ye sacred witts with your celestiall artes,
despise ech muse, science will not prevaile; 16
ffor neither *Mars*, nor sweet *Mineruas* quill,
cann reape reward in his longe practised skill. 18

Then woe to vertue! woe our miscreant daies! 19
thrice woe to them whome vertue doth adorne!
faire *Crisopeia* with her goulden Rayes,
ech wight of worth doth taunt with bitinge scorne, 22
for vertue looseth what she well deserveth,
hee onelie gaines, who *Crisopeia* serueth. 24

without her bewtie, none maie favour praye; 25
without her meane, all labour is in vaine;
vertue, stand back, vnles shee make the waie;
valour and learninge, give place vnto her trayne. 28
thus, muse, far well thow seest thy fatall ende,
faire *Crisopeia* will not bee thy frende. 30

[leaf 41] (3) Vpon the armed Statue of Venus.

ffayre *Venus*, tell whye dost thow Armor beare, 1
and cloggs thy self with heavie Coate of Steele;
thow art not *Mars*, thoughe his attire thow weare,
nor warlick broyles thow ever yet didst feele; 4
sweet speech, good lookes, allurements of delight,
are weapons servinge better for thy fight. 6

In vaine, therfore, thus feircelie art thow armed, 7
for natures harnesse best beseemes thy kinde;
with blowdie weapons why shouldest thow be charmed,
wherin small comfort thow dost ever finde? 10
for naked and vnarm'd, with bewties sheilde
thow madest the god of battell for to yeilde. 12

(4) Sundrie and strange effectes of wyne.

The drunken menn, whome gluttonie doth fill
with wynes excesse, doe sundrie passions houlde:
the one lookes highe, and will not be controlde;
one other singes with loftie voice and shrill; 4

one other mournes, shedding teares manifolde ;
with blasphemie, some one his sowle doth kill. 6

Somme one, with stretched hands to god doth praye ; [leaf 41, back]
one, as his humor is, seekes peace to make ; 8
one other, noe man for his frend doth take ;
one nimblie dances, or ells doth skipp and playe ;
somme, verses write, for their swete Ladies sake,
and summ for hast doe often loose their waye. 12

Summ cannot speake, sum stammer at ech worde, 13
summ whoope and hallowe, and braye with open throte ;
summ, filthie talke doe vse in bawdries note ;
one doth dispute till hee laye vnder borde ; 16
mongst brambells summ runn, till they teare there coate,
summ frett and fume, and naught but blowes afford. 18

One falls to Lecherous actes, like beaste, past shame ;
annother cannot hould himself from sleepe ;
summ other rowles his eyes like mased sheepe ;
summ finde greate faultes, and others moe doe blame; 22
somme, for his life cannot his counsell keepe,
and somm backbite all others with defame. 24

One, as he goeth, endenteth with his feete ; 25
one gapes and yawnes, stretchinge his slothfull arme ;
one thinkes he is a witch, and straight doth charme ;
one other scoffes at ech whome he doth meete ; 28
one other spues out right, but thinkes noe harme ; [leaf 42]
and some therebye with death and sicknes meete. 30

which severall force, in wyne is never founde, 31
for simplie of it self it works noe ill,
but shewes what humors doth the person fill,
and what conceites doe in his braines abounde 34
yf hee doe gorge it in at his owne will,
vntemperatlie his sences for to wounde.
 Then yf thy self thow wilt not once bewraye,
 Shonn wynes excesse, which takes thy witts awaye. 38

(5) Contemninge.

Whoe doeth contempne the worlds fond vanitie, 1
whoe doth contempne that fleshly part of his,
whoe doth contempne no man in miserie,
and doth contempne that hee contempned is: 4
by these contemptes shall make himself regarded,
and at the last with heavenlie Ioyes rewarded. 6

whoe doth contempne religion and her sawes, 7
whoe doth contempne correction of his will,
whoe doth contempne the prince, the crowne, the lawes,
[leaf 42, back] and doth contempne the helpe of learned skill: 10
by these contemptes, to his reproche doth gaine
hate, shame, and greife, with everlastinge payne. 12

---

(6) What maketh menn forgett themselues.

Alluring bewtie, with her cristall face, 1
the heate of youth enflaminge loftie minde,
the favour of the people, and their grace,
the greate presumption of the strength wee find, 4
the store of wealth, the pride of hawtie harte,
and swelling skill of learning and of arte, 6

The Princes love (protecting of our will), 7
the stubborne furie of disturbed brayne,
eager desire for to revenge our will,
and fretting envie with scornefull disdaine, 10
makes vs forgett our selves, and takes awaye
sweet reasons vse, our onelie helpe & staye. 12

---

(7) Thinges not to be recalled.

The stone once cast out of the hand or slinge,
the tyme once past consuming everie thinge,
[leaf 43] the foolishe wordes w*hi*ch throughe the lipps doe flie,
the broken *Hymen* of virginitie, 4

by witt, by art, by pleasure, or by paine,
cannot returne, or ells be calld againe.
then well foresee, before thy hand doe ought,
spend not the goulden tyme on things of naught,   8
premeditate before thow speake in haste,
doe keepe thy bodie allwaies cleane and chaste;
Soe shalt thow live free from the worlds distresse,
and in thy self thy self full well possesse.   12

---

(8) The vnapt not to be forced to learninge.

To *Salamanca* yf thow send an Asse,   1
to *Oxford, Cambridge, Paris*, or dowaye, [Douai]
or that by travell to farthest lands hee passe,
or in the princes Court longe tyme doe staye: 4
yf, when he went, he were an Asse, noe art
will make him horse, for felde, for waie, for cart.   6

Then spare your cost, yf nature give not witt,   7
to send your sonns vnto the learned scooles,
for to the same, yf nature make not fitt,
doe what you cann, they still shall prove but fooles;   10
then tourne ech witt to that which nature will,   [leaf 43, back]
els fondlie thow thy sonne and cost dost spill.   12

---

(9) The waye to gett and keepe frendes.

ffyne witts, much art, sweet tongues, and flatterie,   1
doe gaine and keepe vs frendes, as some men saye;
but these are vaine, as proofe doth testifie,
without large giftes, which makes the readie waye;   4
for though that *Homer* come with learned hande,
yf naught he give, without dores maie he stande.   6

This then must be the surest grounde, I finde,   7
to winn and hould such frends as wee desire:

first give thow much, be plyant to their minde,
take naught of others, fewe thinges doe thow require, 10
which if with heed thow wiselie dost retayne,
a heape of frends thow worthilie shalt gayne. 12

Wee all doe love to take, as *Ioue* doth teach, 13
which dailie guiftes and sacrifice doth crave;
Nonn loue to give, but such as cannot reach
the full effect of that which they would haue; 16
trust *Ouid* then, whoe spake what he did knowe:
it shewes great witt, large giftes for to bestowe. 18

[leaf 44] ## (10) Of Stumblinge.

The prowde horse that treades with statelie pace, 1
and champes his foming mouth on goulden bitt,
adorn'd with curious trapping and pleasant grace,
of his braue looke his humor for to fitt, 4
with his fower feet, when hee doth prance and playe,
stumbles and falls in Iourneyeng of the waye. 6

What marvayle then, though worldlie men and proude, 7
adorn'd with sacred reason of the minde,
In whome the heavens and earth themselves doe shrowd,
with his twoo feet, as nature hath assign'd, 10
In Iournyeng to the place of heavenlie Ioye,
doth fall and stumble, through the worlds annoye! 12

---

(11) First guestes at a feaste.

The buzzinge flye which falls in everie thinge, 1
the meger dogg that hopes to gorge his mawe,
the wandring mynstrell, redie for to singe,
the roaging beggar living without lawe, 4
the Parasite smell-feast, which newes doth bringe,
and cares not whome his flattring tongue doth stinge,
[leaf 44, back] allthough vnbidd, like vnto shameles beastes,
with hast come first vnto all solempne feastes. 8

(12) When a wife is badd, worse, and worst.
When she is good, better, and beste.

My frend, yf that my Iudgement do not fayle,   1
as one well taught by longe experience skill,
thy wife allwaies is but a needefull ill,
and beste is bad, thoughe faire she beare her saile,   4
but vs'd not well, she worser is to thee,
but worst of all when best she seemes to bee.   6

Thy wife is good when shee forsakes this light,   7
and yealdes by force to natures destinie,
she better is (thowe livinge) yf she die,
but best when shee doth soonest take her flight,   10
for soe to thee thine ease shee doth restore,
which soonest hadd, doth comforte thee the more.   12

---

(13) A Puritane.

Dame *Lais* is a puritane by religion,   1
Impure in her deedes, though puer in her talke,
And therefore a puritane by condition,   3 [leaf 45]
or pluritane, which after manie doth walke;
for pruritie of wemenn, by lecherous direction,
seekes pluritie of men to worke satisfaction.   6

---

(14) Of heauie and light.

Philosophers were fooles, that taught of ould   1
that naught cann worke his natures contrarie,
Since experience (best proofe) hath them controld,   3
that heavie makes light, and light makes heavie;
for a light purse makes a heavie harte, wee finde,
and heavie purse doth make light hart and minde.   6

(15) Waterhowse.

With milder sport, and not with bitter speech,   1
licence me here with thee somewhat to playe.
doe take it well, I frendlie thee beesech,
I thinke but mirth what soe my penn bewraye,   4
not meaning the t'offend in anie waye,
vpon thy name, allthough my penn do straye.   6

for since with *Bacchus* Iuice thine inward part   7
is dailie moystened, for thine owne delighte,
[leaf 45, back] and that the blood of Earth revives thy hart,
clensinge thy sowles howse both daie and night,   10
thow rather 'wynehowse,' for thy livelie spright,
then 'waterhowse,' shouldst termed be of right.   12

---

(16) A preist which knewe not anie letter.

Good zealous preist, thy hart more than thy skill,
thy zeale more than thy learning or thy witt,
the sacred eares of mightie *Ioue* must fill,
or ells for god thow wilt be nothing fitt.   4

Of holie Pawle, yet thow the heavenlie voice
cannst ringe alowd, and sound this sentence true,
'the Letter kills,' wherby thow maiest reioyce,
that of one Letter the forme thow never knewe.   8

ffor least that this deade letter should thee kill,
thow didst beware the letters for to learne,
and that aptlie, since of godds holie will
the quickning spirrit thow never couldst deserne.   12

[leaf 46]   ## (17) The hedd and the tayle.

Great was the glorious fame, most worthie knight,   1
stout *Perseus*, when with thy warlike knife
thow strakest of the monsters hedd, in sighte
of vglie *Gorgon*, then bereav'd of life;   4
but farr more famous should haue byn thy glorie
yf thow hadst cutt of the tayles of the Clergie.   6

(18) Cause of a deere yeare.

Thow fondlie askest me, as though I were a god,
what causeth this continued dearth, and plague of Ioue
    his rod.
yf I the truth maie tell, although it purchase blame,
I will not spare to speake my thought, but yet to thy
    defame :   4
Th'inseasonable yeare, this dearth doth not procure,
nor the discurtesie of heauen, w*hi*ch thus wee doe Indure,
nor *Saturns* cursed starr, nor barraynesse of land,
nor want of heedie carefullnes of things wee haue in
    hand,   8
nor *Ioue* his iust anger powr'd out on mortall wightes
for these our manie heaped sinns, and for the fleshe
    delights ;
but thow dost plague vs all, and force vs for to die,
through murdring death, and famins rage, by thy
    extremitie ;   -   12
for since the greedie mawes of thee, thy sonns and kinne,
cann never well be satisfied with that they dailie winn,
but that they horde, they scrape and gripe all that they   [leaf 46, back]
    maie,
to sett them selues in highe estate by euerie manns decaye,
devouring all the paynes w*hi*ch others doe imploye,
howe maie it chuse, but derth and want, all others
    must destroye ?   18

---

(19) Pinkes.

ffreind *Meering*, I deeme you smell verie sweete,
that are soe full of Pinkes from hedd to the feete ;
Yet if euerie Pinke of yo*u*r hatt, doblet, and hose   3
were decked with a garden Pinke to savo*u*r your nose,
You might stand for a maye game, what so you do thinke ;
for thoughe the flowers were sweet, yo*u*r follie wold
    stinke.   6

(20) Shoinge.

Good Browne, thow doest complaine with heavie cheere,
the Shomaker shoes thee not to thy minde.
the fault is not his, as it maie appeare,
that with straite shoes thy foote hee doth bynde, 4
for hee makes them small like thy foote in ech thinge,
since, in shooing thee, hee must shooe a goslinge. 6

---

(21) Glasses.

[leaf 47] The sundrie sort of glasses which art doth put in vre
for our delights, in severall kindes, sweete pleasures doe
procure:
the daintie Ladies, loue in lookinge glasse to prye; 3
the glasse perspective, is desyrd of learnd Pholosophie;
greate states, their windowes deck with glasse, for their
delight;
the searchinge Chimists, for their art, haue glasses
strange of sight;
the burning glasse is made, a thinge of rare devise;
and glasse vessells for banquettinge are dailie had in
pryse; 8
besides, there is of glasse a temple faire and brighte,
which learned Chaucer builded hath with penn of
heavenlie spright;
And gascoigne, for his sport, hath made a glasse in verse,
wher wee maie see our owne defaults, which there he
doth reherse; 12
but all these curious glasses, or anie of like kinde,
or other strange proportion which art or wealth maie finde,
Cannot content my frende; hee hath them in disdayne,
hee them reiects as frivolous, he houlds them all in
vayne, 16
for, of all sorts of glasse which give forth anie shine,
my frend loues, euerie hower, to haue a venice glasse of
wyne. 18

(22) One assured he was elected.

Thow greatlie bragst how that thow art
    assur'd thow art elected :
Chaunge but one letter, and thow saiest true,   [leaf 47, back]
    because thow art eiected.   4
ffor, knocking at the heavenlie gate,
    to enter as right heire,
Thow art repulsd as bastard childe,
    and driven to deepe despaire.   8

(23) Cham.

In all the course of thy vnhappie yeares,   1
noe kinde of vertue in thy life appeares ;
ffor thow art *Cham*, or ells *Chamms* wicked brother :
he did deride his father; and thow thy mother ;   4
his curse was greate ; and soe will fall to thee,
that scoffes at her which still should honnored bee.   6

(24) Fayth.

Our Saviour *Christ*, with words of greife complayned,
that when he came to Iudge the world by fyer,
that fayth should not be found to his desire,
soe greatlie should the Christian fayth be strayned.   4
but if he nowe the same would come to finde,
he should see faythes more then stande with his minde ;
ffor greater and more faiths in yearth,   [leaf 48]
    with menn did not abounde,   8
Soe contrarie, soe confident,
    soe pleasant to bee founde.   10

(25) Cuttinge of tyme.

The Curious gardiner, with his cruell Shires   1
doth cutt the wholsome tyme, and her sweet flowers ;
which hee doth cutt soe longe, till tyme at length
cuts of his life by doome of heavenlie powres,   4

for tyme, in tyme cutts him with full despight,
that first by tyme cutt tyme from his delight.   6

(26) A tench and a wench.

A Catholike and a Protestant   1
   were frendlie sett at meate,
for both whose dinner was prepared,
   both fyshe and fleshe to eate.   4
They both, as did their conscience bidd,
   feed on the severall dishe :
The Protestant vpon the fleshe,
   the Papist on the fishe.   8
[leaf 48, back] At length the Catholike complaind,
   our wantoun times to bee
disordered in everie thinge,
   as dailie hee did see :   12
'ffor nowe our Protestants,' (said hee,)
   'which newe Religion take,
Twixt Pigg and Pike, twixt Carpe and Capon,
   not anie difference make.'   16
To whome the other replied : 'wee make
   such difference of their kinde
As Papists doe twixt tench and wench,
   to serve their wantoun minde.'   20

(27) Whoe are happie.

Antomedon the *Greeke Poet* doth tell,   1
and rightlie, yf the same be wayed well,
that firste he happie mann is sayed to bee,
which oweth nought, and is from borrowinge free ;   4
Next, hee whome wedlocks fetters doth not strayne ;
the third, whome childrens cares did never payne.
but if he bee soe madd to take a wife,
to ridd himself from his most quiet life,   8
yf shee be rich, and therwith soone to die,
hee happie is, to gaine her wealth therbye.   10

(28) Linguistes. [leaf 49]

Twoe gentlemen at meate by enterchaunge
of frendlie speech, the tyme to entertayne,
a womann did commend for vertues straunge,
as one that too much learning did attaine, 4
being a greate linguist, whych praise doth gaine;
for of the tongues shee nothinge was to seeke,
since she was skill'd in Hebrew and in Greeke.
The other said, "marveyle not much 8
   that they such cuninge take,
ffor nature, by a speciall grace,
   great linguists doth them make." 11

(29) Drinkinge.

The first delightinge draught
   doth well thy Pallat please;
The second doth thy hart comfort,
   and thy could stomake ease. 4

The third doth make the pleasant wyne
   well knowne vnto thy skill;
The fourth encreaseth suddaine mirth,
   and pleasure doth distill. 8

The fifte the braine doth heate, [leaf 49, back]
   throwout in everie parte;
The sixte doth make the[e] verie learn'd
   and cuninge in ech art. 12

The seaventh makes the[e] like [a] horse
   that runnes without a rayne;
The eight, thy sences doth confound,
   and takes awaye thy brayne. 16

The ninth doth make the[e] like
   a swyne to fyle the place;
The tenth doth make thee worse then madd,
   and hated with disgrace. 20

Then flye excesse of wyne,
  which is not worthie blame,
ffor thow, not that, doste cause this ill,
  to thy perpetuall shame.   24

---

(30) Enuye.

Thow monster of mankinde, obscurer of good name,
thow hated childe of pride, and autor of thy shame,
whose heares are stinging snakes, whose face is pale & wann,
with scornfull eyes and browes, disdaining euerie mann,
with canker taynted tethe, and poysoned tongue of spight,   5
with vile detracting lipps, defaming euerie wighte,
[leaf 50] with breth of Sulphures smell, fedd with revenges desire,
with brests defyld with gall, and hart of flaminge Ire,
whose nayles are harpies clawes, and bodie leane and spare,   9
which never smiles, beinge still opprest with greife & care,
whose frettinge pynes thy hart, and eates thy flesh awaie,
still feeding on thy self, till thow dost cleane decaye 12
like burning *Aetna* monte, which with his stinking fumes
feedes on it self, and with his flame it self consumes.
thy force ech sowle doth feele, thoughe, to thy better paine, 15
except the mann deiect, whome fortune doth disdaine.

---

(31) Mann must provide for bodie and sowle.

The fairest Creature which the heavenlie hand   1
created, hath the cheefest thinge hee made,

the Lord of Ayre, of Earth, of sea, and Land,
and of ech earthlie thinge which once must fade, 4
composed is of bodie form'd of claye,
and sowle divine which never shall decaye. 6

His sacred minde, sprung from celestiall seede, 7
doth him forwarne to lifte the same on hie.
his earthlie bodie, which elements doth feede,
makes him to thinke on thinges, and that be worldlie.
Thus sowle and bodie, vnited by their kinde, [leaf 50, back]
makes mann both heaven and earth allwaies to mind.

But soe to minde them both, as not excesse 13
in either, fall contrarie to their due,
for all extreames, the vice doth still expresse,
the (meane) is that which wee ought to pursue; 16
then, since god wilbe serv'd with both together,
vse well the one, to helpe and serve the other. 18

---

(32) Mongers.

A messe of mongers on *Holborne hill*, 1
the dolefull waie vnto the hatefull place,
where malefactors, much against their will,
cutt of their times with shame and fowle disgrace, 4
were frendlie mett, ech other faire greetinge,
asking what craft ech vsed for his livinge. 6

One said he was of the ffellmongers trade; 7
one other, that he Ironmonger was;
the thirde, that hee was costardmongers Iade;
the fourth, that he was a ffishmongers asse; 10
to whome a fifte, as by them he did walke,
with listening eare enclining to their talke, 12

did saye, "exclude me not, I craue, from out the rest, [leaf 51]
for of your trade I am the Quintessence, 14
since I am a monger good as the best,
and of my fleshe and purse, of Lardge dispence." 16

"what monger maiest thow bee," did one replie,
"vnknowne as yett to all this companie?" 18
fforthwith the mann, as pertest of them all, 19
sayed hee a whoremonger was knowne to bee;
"I will not loose my place in mongers hall,
being prentise once, although I now be free." 22
then all shooke hands, as nere of kinde to other,
biddinge him wellcome as their loving brother;
whoe, to confirme this knott of knaverie,
vnto the taverne hasted spedilie. 26

(33) Tyme.

An Auncient knight of ffee and of renowne,
with his Ladie to dinner sate him downe:
they sett; the hungrie knight did bid his mann
some pottage sett, with which the knight begann; 4
but eatinge fast and over greedilie,
a little herbe did take his course awrye,
[leaf 51, back] which made him coffe, that chok'd he was, he said.
Yet the good Ladie, therwith not dismayed, 8
"Sir, it is tyme, it is but tyme," replied.
the payned knight, the more, for anger, cried
that chok'd he was; but his Ladie, that ment
but well, saied "it is but tyme, sir, be content!" 12
whereat the knight the more did coffe and strayne,
ffor Anger of her speech then of the payne;
for where her wordes the herbe tyme did intend,
hee them mistooke, and deem'd shee sought his ende,
since wronglie hee conceiv'd therbye that shee
thought it but tyme that he should choked bee. 18

(34) Receipts and expenses.

A tutor, gluttinous and prodigall,
was by the Iudge assigned to a pupill,
who in excesse and ryot spendinge all,
with daintie fare his hungrie mawe did fill. 4

The Iudge, offended with this lewde expence,
wilde the tutor a good accompt to make;
but he replied, without all reverence,
"there is naught left, and this count must you take." 8

The Angrie Iudge perceyvinge this deceipt, [leaf 52]
would knowe what he receyu'd and howe twas spent:
the tutor, gaaping, said, "her's the receyte
and her's th'expence," notinge his hinder vente. 12

---

(35) Counterfetts deuoure the whole world.

The kinge deuoures the husbandman;
  fond youths do spoyle the kinge;
The vsurer consumes those youthes.
  the preist decaye doth bringe   4
To vsurers; and whores consume
  the preist with filthie lust;
The bawd eates vp the gayninge whore
  who putteth her in truste;   8
The taverner beggars the bawde;
  and next is swallowed vpp
The taverner, by Parasites
  which hange vpon the cupp.   12
The needie Parasites in th'end
  are spoyled by lothed lyce;
The Ape, mann counterfetter, eates
  those vermyn at a trice.   16
So that the beastlie, mocking Ape,
  which mowes at everie thinge,
By circulation doth consume   [leaf 52, back]
  the kingedome and the kinge.   20

---

(36) That one thinge Produceth annother.

The frutefull peace begetts desired plentie;   1
desired plentie brings forth lothsome pride;

the lothsom pride makes men by warr to die;
longe warrs cause wofull povertie ech tyde, 4
and povertie makes frutefull peace to springe:
thus the worlds wheele is turn'd in everie thinge. 6

The fruitfull earth gives forth sustayning grasse; 7
sustayning grasse doth feed the norishing beasts;
the nourishing beaste, into manns flesh doth passe;
and glotinous mann, that feedes with daintie feaste, 10
dissolved is to frutefull yearth in hast;
for what feede vs, one vs doth feed at last. 12

Thus runns about by dailie circulation 13
ech earthlie thinge create by heavenlie hand;
for ones curruption is others generation,
as natures lawe hath linked with her band; 16
then happie thow, if sowle in true degree
doe end in god, from whome it came to thee. 18

[leaf 53] (37) A longe nose.

A knight that should with curtesie
   a ladie entertayne,
at her longe nose begann to scoffe
   with words of some disdaine, 4
and said, 'yf your longe nose were not
   a bulwarke of defence
To gard your lipps, they should be kiss'd
   before wee parted hence.' 8
'why, sir,' quoth shee, 'spare not therfore,
   yf nose such hindrance bee,
you maie, where hindred nose doth want,
   with ease freelie kisse mee.' 12
The scoffing knight thus retaunted,
   in furie flange awaye,
But with replyeng scoffe before,
   he thus to her did saye: 16

'Madame, it greatlie forceth not,
    for sweetnes of yo*u*r breth,
Whether I kisse yo*u*r lipps above,
    or ells yo*u*r hipps beneath.'   20

(38) Spencers Fayrie Queene. [leaf 53, back]

Renowmed Spencer, whose heavenlie sprite   1
ecclipseth the sonne of former poetrie,
in whome the muses harbor w*i*th delighte,
gracinge thy verse w*i*th Immortalitie,   4
Crowning thy fayrie Queene w*i*th deitie,
the famous *Chaucer* yealds his Lawrell crowne
vnto thy sugred penn, for thy renowne.   7

Noe cankred envie cann thy fame deface,   8
nor eatinge tyme consume thy sacred vayne;
noe carpinge zoilus cann thy verse disgrace,
nor scoffinge Momus taunt the w*i*th disdaine,   11
since thy rare worke eternall praise doth gayne;
then live thou still, for still thy verse shall live,
to vnborne poets, wh*i*ch light and life will give.   14

(39) Martine.

Menn say thow art call'd the Rich Martine,   1
in Latiane speech who art Martinus nam'de;
but wholie they mistake thie name, I wynne,
if to thy gaine the same be dulie fram'd,   4
for Martinus thow shouldst be termed right,
in hording gould wh*i*ch hast soe greate delight.   6

(40) Vsurers. [leaf 54]

Stukelie the vsurer is dead, and bid vs all farwell,
who hath a Iourney for to ride vnto the court of hell;
yf anie would his letters send to Plutoes divelishe grace,
hee wilbe messenger therfore, and beare them to that
    place;   4

but yf he anie answer crave, of letters sent from hence,
he must some other post provide, which maie returne
    from thence,
for *Stukelie* once arived there, cannot come back againe,
since *Pluto*, for his needfull vse, doth meane him to
    retaine.   8

(41) Grace.

A man of lewd living all vertue sett at naught,
was rested by Sergiant at mace, and vnto prison brought,
who beinge sett at large, the *Bishop* would him trye,
and him to common pennance put, for dedes of
    Lecherie.   4
his aged mother, greved of her sonns open shame,
with gentle speech of moothers loue, his lewd follies did
    blame,
and said 'that want of grace did force him soe to fall;
wherfore hee dailie, on his knees, for needfull grace
    must call.'   8
her scoffinge sonne, which scorn'd his mother with dis-
    daine,
said 'hee would rather hang, than seeke for anie grace
    againe;
for seriaunt grace his mace, his purse had sucked drie,
and the Archbishopps reverend grace had sham'd him
    penlie;   12
[leaf 54, back] And therefore since these twoo before, him did deface,
he soe, past grace, bequeath[d] them both vnto the
    divells grace.'   14

(42) Cardinge.

Kate is a good huswife, as all men saye,
for shee doth nought but card all the longe daie,
whoe in continuall carding hath such delight,
that, besides the daie, she will card in the night.   4

ffor cardinge, to her is but a pleasant playe,
and when she playes she is cardinge allwaies.
Yet by her carding she hath little winninge,
for of her carding never com[e]th spinninge ; 8
Soe she is a huswife, but noe good huswife, I trowe,
for of good huswifes cardinge, spinning doth growe.

(43) Reelinge.

Iohn, thy wife, to live doth take great payne, 1
a good huswifes name therbye to gaine ;
for she spinnes and Reeles as fast as shee maye,
but cheeflie in reelinge spending the daye ;
for, once haue shee sett the pott at her hedd,
she never lins reelinge till shee goe to bedd. 6

(44) A Rose. [leaf 55]

Willford, thow lovest a pleasant Rose verie well,
both for the faier cullor and the sweete smell,
for thow canst not bee without a rose in thy bedd,
to colle the, and to laye her arme vnder thy hedd. 4
Yet is not thy *Rose*, flower of Carnation hue,
nor perfect white, nor redd, but yellowishe and blewe,
and therfore most meete to serve in the night, 7
for other Roses would shame her if she were in the light.

(45) Sowinge.

Sweete flowers growe when gardeners sowes the seed ;
the plowman sowes the graine wherby wee live ;
and man sowes that wheron mankinde doth breed,
soe that their sowing, his like doth allwaies give. 4

But weemen sowe farr different from these kindes,
both workes and wordes which send forth paine and
    greefe,
for with there words they vex their husbands mindes,
with needle sowinge, not gayninge their releife. 8

They sowe discorde, with tongue of false report;
their needle sowinge, doth breed but more expence;
they sowe deceyt, and make therof a sport;
their needle workes are but a showes pretence.   12
[leaf 55, back] Then lett not wemenn sowe, yf thow bee quiet bent,
for of their doble sowing, growes naught but discontent.

(46) Woodcocks.

He is as wise as a Woodcock, all wee doe see,
because everie woodcock is as wise as hee,
w*hi*ch wee knowe to be true, and that the rather,
for that Alderman woodcock was his father :   4
A thinge of greate worth, that woodcocks are made
the governours of Citties and the Marchants trade.
Then woodcock on his side, by birth and by witt,   7
makes him as wise as a woodcock his birth for to fitt;
for if naught ells causd him a woodcock to bee,
yet since he is borne a woodcock in everie degree,
he cannot degenerate from woodcocks kinde,   11
and therfore as wise as a woodcock you shall him finde.

(47) Kissinge.

Three pleasant gentlemen vpon the waye
did meete three maides that went them forth to playe;
the menn of ech other would gladlie knowe,
w*hi*ch of the maides he would kisse in the rowe.   4
the maydes, like goselinges, after other went,
noe whit mindinge the menn nor their intent.
But of the menn, the first amongst the rest,
[leaf 56] that with his fellowes scoffinglie would Iest,   8
said 'hee would kisse the pretie maide before,'
not meaning for to meddle w*i*th anie more.
the other said, 'yf he might haue his wishe,
the browne wench in the middle he would kisse;'   12

the third, as liked best vnto his minde, 13
said 'hee would kisse the blobcheckt wench behinde.'
Nowe, fellow *Garrett*, of the would I crave,
which of these three the sweetest kisse should haue;
for the wenches breath, formost of the three, 17
smelled verie ranke in the highest degree.

(48) White heares.

At the Rose within newgate, ther frendlie did meete,
fower of my ould frends, ech other for to greete :
one had a black beard, but white was his hedd ;
one other, white hedd, with a beard which was redd ;
the third had yellowish hedd, but his beard somewhat
    white ; 5
the yongest had silver berde, and hedd agreeing righte.
thus sett at their cupps, they thought to devise
howe these severall white heares in them did arise. 8
the black berd and white hedd begann for to saye,
'his hedd was elder then his berde by twentie winters
    daye,
ffor where nature by age doth soonest decaye, [leaf 56, back]
graye heares spring vp, which age doe displaye.' 12
the other white hedd with the reddishe beard, tould,
'that his hedd was not white because he was ould,
but for that he had more labored, by studie his brayne,
then his teeth by eatinge, his hedd white heares did
    gayne.' 16
the third, with yellowish hedd and beard somwhat white,
Philosopher-like, this cause did recite,
' I see it perfect true, for soe you agree,
that what is labored most will weakest bee ; 20
and what of mann is most weake by kinde,
soonest graye haires in that part you shall finde ;
then vsinge my teeth more than my witt, by right,
my berde then my witt, must needes be more white.'

the last, with a ieste to knitt vp the game, 25
this reason for himself begann for to frame,
' hornes and hoore hares comm not by age, menn tell,
and that by my self I haue tried verie well,
for havinge both agreeing together, 29
Cares gaue the one, and my wife gaue the tother.'

(49) Cutters.

' Iack, I here thow hast leaft thine ould trade;
thow wilt noe more become a ripiers Iade.'
[leaf 57] ' In fayth, good Will, thow sayest true,
for I haue left mine ould occupation for a newe, 4
for I cann braue it in the streetes with the rest,
beinge a right cutter, as good as the best.'
' A cutter! what cutter, I praye the, maye that bee?
a cutter of Queene hithe, or a garment cutter, tell mee, 8
A Swashebuckler cutter, or one of the cutthrotes,
or a garden cutter, or a false cutter of groates?
Or art thow such a cutter as ostelers and tapsters be,
or a woode cutter, a stone cutter, or a heare cutter, letts
see?' 12
noe, in faith, Will, for better or worse,
I am none of these, but a plaine cutpurse;
a life of such pleasinge, that I never feele payne
till the rope and the gallowes doe hinder my gaine.' 16

(50) The deceased Pretor.

Thy vertue, not thy vice; faith, not dissembling speech;
thy goodnes, not thy flowings goods, made thee this
honor reach.

(51) To Humfrie Waldronn.

Yf reasons worthie minde prescribe this reede, 1
and Iustice bidd ech one with Iust desart

for to requite with like, the frendlie deede,
in outward shewe and inward faithfull harte, 4
then must I yeald vnto your gentle heste, [leaf 57, back]
and streyne my quill to answere your request. 6

Wherin with slender phrase I gentlie craue 7
your skillfull muse to pardon skillesse write,
and rather waie the honnest minde I haue,
then simple quill which rashelie doth recite 10
what Idle brayne hath fondlie found at large,
which I present, our freindshipp to discharge. 12

A ffoolishe *Cherill* I maye seeme to bee, 13
that shame not to present vnto thy sight
Sir Topas ridinge rime not meet for thee,
Nor Gouldings learned vewe, that famous wight, 16
whose hawtie verse, with sugredd words well knitt,
bereaves the same of *Chawcers* flowing witt.
Then frendlie take in gree this frendlie verse I frame,
and thinke, to his *Perithous*, that *Thesius* writes the
same. 20

(52) Fortune.

Blinde ffortune, with her fonde and sencelesse sence,
regarding nought the worth of anie wight,
which heedleslie her riches doth dispence,
not forcinge whether shee doth wronge or right, 4
Enricht by suche as vices do adorne,
The good reiectinge with most bitter skorne, [leaf 58]
Which growes, for that noe perfect good she knowes,
beinge onelie fedd with vaine and outward showes. 8

(53) To his freind Burrell.

The loathed povertie still shall thee feede
yf poore thow be in anie time of life,
By byrth, or fortune, or for want of heede,
for vnto such, rewards are nothinge rife, 4

since, in this thanklesse age, none wealth attaine,
but such as riches haue, and giue for gaine.
Then must thy hard and woefull state
    of shamefast povertie   8
Embrace patience, since vnto thee
    welth will not multiplie.

(54) Issues.

The Ioyfull mother brings forth manie faire yssues,
the learned lawyer brings his cause to good yssues,
the skilld Phisition makes for goute runninge yssues,
the faulting Iuror is amerc'd in much yssues ;   4
the large expences are counted needles yssues ;
but yet, of all the yssues wee haue in anie kinde,
none is more badd then yssuing from our land, wee finde,
for soe our witt and wealth from vs soone yssues then, 8
which lost and brought to naught, w'are scorned of all
    menn :
[leaf 53, back] Such yssue they obteyne, their birth right which doe sell,
on which yssue the verdit hath condempned mee right
    well.

(55) Mariage.

Deepe witted menn, b'experience haue contrived,   1
that mariage good and quiet is ech hower,
where the mans heringe organs are deprived
of their right vse and sound receyving power,   4
and where is seeled vp the womans percing sights
that shee maie not behould her husbands sweet delights. 6

ffor since nature hath made that sex most fraile,   7
and subiect to tormentinge Ielousie,
vpon ech guiltles signe they will not fayle,
their loving husbands to suspect falselie ;   10
yet if she could not see, but were by nature blinde,
such fonde conceites she would not harbor in her minde.

And if suspected mann were dombe to heere 13
the Iealous brawles of his vnquiet wife,
ech would embrace and hould the other deere,
wherbye they might obtayne a quiet life, 16
without which rare effects, swete mariage is a hell,
but linked with these guiftes, doth Paradice excell. 18

(56) Sweete mouthes. [leaf 59]

A noble Earle, to vertue allwaies bent,
with rich and scoffinge knight on hunting went:
the Buck was rows'd, the hounds vncopled bee,
who with swifte course, to flie did seeme to mee, 4
and eger of the game, in their full crie
with dobled voice lowd ecchoed in the skie,
whose pleasant musick did the eares delight
of Earle and all the rest, except the knight, 8
that pleasured more in purchasing and gayne
than hawkes or hounds, or in such toyes vaine.
of whome the Earle demanded curteouslie,
when ended was the hounds long solempne crie, 12
'yf those faire doggs, with their reioicing voice,
had not sweete mouthes as hounds of rarest choice;'
wherto the knight gaue answere scoffinglie,
'hee did not knowe till hee the same should trie, 16
for anie of them he never kissed there,
and soe knewe not how sweet that there mouthes were.'
wherat good Earle, which tooke it in disdaine,
from moved chollar hardlie could refraine, 20
but said 'if that you kist them not before,
you maie with ease kisse them behinde the more.'

(57) Fooles. [leaf 59, back]

Hee was not wise, his witt hath him deceyved, 1
that would bee wise, and not a foole be deemed,

but I, which haue the truth by witt conceyved,
doe holde it best a foole to bee estemed, 4
the cause wherof by reason is perceyved,
ffor wisdome knowes, of fooles is endlesse number,
that in their follie foolishlie doe slumber. 7

Then is it best to be of that consort 8
and sweete societie which moste doe hould;
the fewest menn to wisdome doe resort,
and leste in number soonest are contrould; 11
soe least are least estem'd in everie sort;
then must the wise, which is the lesser number,
be compted those which all the world doe cumber. 14

Greate ffranchises the fooles are knowen to haue, 15
because they swaye in all the greatest part:
the wise stand back, forc't of the fooles to crave,
thoughe fooles cannot Iudge of their good deserte, 18
yet must those fooles their vertuous life deprave,
for they stand warme, are fedd and cloth'd of beste,
when wise menn begg, or are with famin prest. 21

[leaf 60] ## (58) Gallopinge.

ffrom windsore ridinge, to the statelie towne, 1
the seate of ffamous kings and Inglands pryde,
in hast, I mett, in midst of Hunslowe downe,
a gentle youth which postinglie did ride, 4
a frend of mine, whome I forc'd there to staie,
to knowe the cause hee ridd soe fast awaye. 6

Whoe said, "muse not, I frendlie the require, 7
to see mee gallop with soe light a hedd,
since I farr lighter am in this retyre,
then when to *London* I my Iourney spedd; 10
ffor when I went, my creed 12 partes did holde,
but one is lost, soe I more light and bould,
the twelfe is gone, eleaven I keepe in store,
Christ went not vnto hell: what would you more?" 14

(59) Churches.

The Auncient *Saxons* did full Christianlie,
to shewe their fervent zeale and zealous love,
erect most statelie churches plenteouslie,
as holie place ordain'd for god above. 4
But nowe *le monde reuerse*, the world turn'd upside downe,
our *Scismatikes* will haue noe church in Cittie or in towne.
Noe Church! alas! what doe I saye? I lye; ['eaf 60, back]
they sett vpp churches twentie for their one, 8
for everie private howse spirituallie
must bee their church, for other will they none,
Excepte the open felds, or ells false Ethnicks groves of trees,
where sencelesse as the sencelesse woods they flock
like swarms of bees; 12
there sowe they *Satans* damning seedes, of which dissention springs,
(tearing Christes vndivided coate), which all to ruyne
bringes. 14

(60) Menn before Adame.

Good *Moses* (which didst write by sprite of God), 1
some makes thy witt as watrye as thy name;
thy art, to serpents which did turne thy rodd,
thy sacred quill, which newborne world did frame, 4
are nothinge worth; thy Iudgements are but lame;
ffor the *Italian* redie witt doth sett the vnto schoole,
and *Francis George*, in his scriptures problemes, makes
the a foole. 7

Thow couldst not see, (which everie thinge didst see, 8
of newspronge world Create by Ioue his hand,)
that before Adame, (calld first mann by thee,)
were manie menn (which by thy words is skande), 11

for some Italians thy words so vnderstand,
And *Francis George* doth, *Talmude* like,
 by thy penn thee confound,   14
[leaf 61] Provinge that manne *Androgenon*
 was first made out of grownde :
But lett those wranglinge witts, that seeme   17
 to teach godds heavenlie sprite,
Beware his scourging rodd deprive
 them not of sence and light.   20

(61) Iuye.

Thow Bacchus plant, which allwaies greene dost
  springe,   1
Poets reward, and glorie of their penn,
the touchstone of wyne which to the sprite doth bringe
a quickning force to rouse the witt of menn,   4
why dost thow clyme my howse so spreddinglie,
and yeald thy sacredd budds soe frutefullie ?   6

In vaine thow doest ascend these rurall tyles   7
which profound *Virgill* never yet behelde,
nor wantonn *Ouid*, whose rare penn compyles
strange changed shapes which abstruse science yeald, 10
nor wittie *Flaccus* did hange his harpe here,
nor doth *Tibullus* gold in this appere.   12

ffor in this cottage rurall muse doth reste ;   13
here dwelleth *Cherill*, and *Topas* the knighte ;
[leaf 61, back] pore oten ryme is onelie here exprest,
noe helicon verse or muse of rare delight ;   16
but since thow hast this rusticke wall adorned,
doe florishe longe, all though my verse be scorned. 18

(62) Iestinge.

Three things there be which maie susteyne noe Ieste 1
or foolishe blemishe of our Idle braine :

the honest fame wherwith our life is blest;
our godlie faith, for that maye bide noe stayne 4
of heresie, or false religions bayne;
Next, watrishe eye, wherof ech litle gall
doth hurte the sight and dangers th'ye withall. 7

(63) Honor.

The glorious Queene, honor, desir'd of all, 1
wherto ambitious mindes greatlie aspires,
still gapinge, that on them her rayes maye fall
with glorious stiles to answer their desires, 4
which hautie hart by price and prayse requires,
is seldome found, as grave ancients devise,
of such as gredilie wold to honnor rise. 7

ffor shee enquires of those shee never sawe, 8
she followeth them that from her faste doe flye,
she honnors such from her which doe withdrawe, [leaf 62]
she loveth all that naught esteemes her glorie, 11
she calls for them that scorns her vanitie,
she trusteth those whome she did never knowe,
and such rewards in whome hidd vertues flowe. 14
This contemplative Philosophers tould 15
With all their skill, vnknowinge her true kinde;
for other course doth this faire Ladie hould,
since to her glitteringe bowres newe stepps are signed, 18
whertoe nowe none the redie waye cann finde,
but suche as enter with a keye of gould
by false faire shewes or flatteries manifold. 21

(64) Temperance.

The heroike vertues Cardinall,
    wherof the learned write,
Doe from right kinde degenerate,
    and with themselves do fighte. 4

If heavenlie temperance doe not
    their Rygor moderate,
As the true arbitrer and the
    true stickler of their bate.   8

[leaf 62, back] ffor Iustice without temperance
    shadowes revenginge Ire,
And fortitude without the same
    is rashe vnquenched fyre.   12

Soe wisdome wanting the due force
    of temperance, wee trye,
Egregious follie to be deem'de,
    and cosoninge subtiltie.   16

when hee w*hi*ch hath true temperance,
    all vertues doth embrace,
Is wise, is iust, is valiant,
    and honnored in ech place.   20

Since this faire Queene, dame Temperance,
    attended is allwaies
with rare and honnorable maydes
    deserving worthie prayse;   24

ffor lawded virgin modestie,
    and blushefull shamefastnes,
And holie abstinence, the nourse
    of all true godlines,   28

Pure honestie, wise frugallness,
    and right sobrietie,
The Angellike continencie,
    and fames eternitie,   32

[leaf 63] Doe dailie followe Temperance,
    as handmaides ever preste,
And worthie members of that Queene,
    for to performe her heste,   36

Whoe, for their Ladies liverie,
    her ensigne and her worde,
To shewe how her wise actions
    doe with her speech accord.   40

This famous sentence beare vppon
    their sleeves embrodred still
(*Not to much*), which wise *Pitacus*
    fram'd to her sacred will.   44

(65) Doinge nothinge.

A Crabbed Cobler, and his slothfull wife,
which would not labour for to gett her meate,
from words to blowes did often fall at strife;
but as the husband did her feircelie beate,   4
this question shee did oftentimes repeate:
' why doe you thus torment me in my life,
Since I haue nothinge said, nor nothinge donne?'
but he, continuinge still as he begun,   8
Said, 'for that cause onelie he made his blowes soe rife.'

(66) Astrologers. [leaf 63, back]

Malevolent *Saturne*, vnhappie starr,   1
hath loste the vse of ferce and cruell sight,
Ne cann from stone a childe discerne from farre;
the shamefaste moone cann with her bashefull light   4
see naught but what is pure and virgin bright;
the thundringe *Ioue*, with loue doth onelie minde
his white Europa, though a mortall wight;
the warlike *Mars*, to coole his youthfull kinde,   8
doth *Venus* halse; and lustfull *Venus*, *Mars* doth bynde.

The Lawrell *Phebus*, with his glittering hedd,   10
the glorious god that rules in fyerie chaire,
doth onelie thinke on *Daphnes* plesante bedd;
to *Herseus* love, doth *Mercurie* repaire,
the wittie sonne of Maya the faire: 14

thus all the plannetts are employd in skye;
wherbye thow maist (Astrologer) dispaire,
by their aspectes or workinge power, to trye
whoe doth the Cuckold make, and thy hed hornifie. 18

(67) The herbe *filius ante Patrem*.

[leaf G4]
A vertuous Ladie, skilfull herbaliste,
in *Chimick* art whoe takes noe meane delight,
whome modestie with good report hath bliste,
and wifelie dutie hath adorned righte, 4
of gentleman (that learned would bee deem'd,
as by his *tria verba* he had seem'de,)
Demanded 'if the herbe most rare of sight,
and of all Artistes greatlie esteem'de, 8
which *filius ante patrem* they doe hight,
were to him knowne': who said, with courage bould,
his deepe insight in herbes for to vnfould,
'it is, madame, well knowne to everie wight, 12
to be sonne of *Antipater*, as learned men doe houlde.'

(68) Monstrous Childe.

Did Learned *Ouid* live, with poetrie divine,
his Metamorphosis he would a newe refyne,
and add this prodigie, as vncouth as the reste, 3
of his transformed shapes which there he hath expreste;
ffor here, though bodies were to other forms not chang'd,
[leaf G4, back] Yet is this followinge truth as farr from nature strang'd,
That the celestiall saints which doe adorne the skye, 7
should from the heavens discend, and children multiplie;
for why sainte Peters sonne, a thinge to fewe men
        knowne,
maintaind a child which he supposd to bee his owne,
yet others had more righte to her by kindlie knott;
soe easilie one others child falls to our lott. 12
This is a thinge vnvsd, a Saint a sonne to haue,
and hee deformed, not shap'd as heavenlie bodies crave,

whoe, though of heavenlie seed, yet was he foule
    beguylde,
that fondlie nourished as his, one others childe,   16
exceedinge anie chyld which natures course doth give,
for lightlie she could beare the tallest mann on live;
soe bigg her bone in bredth, soe monstrous shee did
    seeme,   19
that ech, noe childe, but perfect woman, did her deeme.
Thus nature changinge kinde,
    these monsters forth doth sende,
Saint Peters sonne, a woman childe,
    which could with menn contende.   24

---

(69) A godly mann.

He is a godlie mann, that doth with tongue and minde
    and sincere hart, the heavenlie god
        adore in his true kinde,
That liberall is to pore, that Iustice doth maintaine,   4   [leaf 65]
    And beinge chosen for a Iudge,
        takes noe reward for gayne;
That is not mov'd with loue, or doth for anger hate,
    And as infectinge poysonn, shunns   8
        fonde scouldinge and debate;
That hath a good foresight in what he takes in hand,
    that rashelie nothinge doth attempte
        which reason maie withstande;   12
That chooseth honnest frends, for to converse with all,
    whose sage and true advise maye helpe
        in dangers when they fall;
That vtters with his tongue, but what his hart conceives,
    And doth envie that wicked speech,   17
        which other menn deceyves;—
This is a godlie mann; but I thinke none is found,
    In whome these sacred vertues doe
        in their full power abounde.   21

(70) Kindred.

Why kneele you heere, faire Ladies, thus amased,　1
　　before *Apollo*, as though you sacrificed?
These litle babes within yo*u*r armes thus foulded,
　　in weepinge sort soe piteouslie disguised?　4
[leaf 65, back] what secret greife of fortunes evill change
　　hath happened you? declare, and bee not straunge.　6

Wee here lament noe fortune of mishapp,　7
wee craue noe goodes from godds for to discende,
ne doe wee wishe our Ennemies to entrapp,
nor seeke revenge of such as vs offende,　10
but of most fowle incest wee feele false fame,
and craue *Apollo* to rid vs from the same.　12

ffor these two babes w*hi*ch here thow dost behould,
are our owne sonns by fleshlie generation;
they are brothers to our husbands, of this be bould,
and vncles to ech other by procreation;　16
their mothers and grandmothers thow shalt vs finde
in lawfull mariage and course of honnest kinde.　18

w*hi*ch wee beseech Apollo for to shewe,　19
who leavinge that to earthlie menn of skill,
wee thee desire, yf ought therof thou knowe,
the same to tell according to our will;　22
Soe shall wee sound thy worth and learned name,
Since thow shalt cleere vs from incestuous shame.　24

[leaf 66]　## (71) The Courte and Cuntrey.

My yonge and youthfull yeares,
　　that once drewe forth my life
In pleasant game of ffancies trayne,
　　where pleasures all were rife,　4
Haue nowe forsaken quite
　　their ould and wonted trade;
My strength is gone, my mirth is past,
　　my wantonn daies doe fade.　8

ffor where I often vsed,
    amongst the Courtlie sort,
In Idle play, through bewties hue,
    with loving talke to sport,   12
Nowe am I shakenn of,
    My faltring tongue doth staye,
Vntimelie thoughts of such mishapp
    hath worne such toyes awaye,   16
And I must rest at home,
    lock'd from my pleasures paste;
They scorne me nowe whome I disdaind:
    this is my fall at laste.   20
ffrom Court to cart I flye,
    a longe but easie leppe;
I liste noe more with glosinge speech   [leaf 66, back]
    on fortunes wheele to stepp.   24
She did advance me once,
    to throwe me downe againe,
But through her spite and my good happ
    more quiet I attaine.   28
The little shrubbs that growe
    hard by the tender grasse,
Abide the force of blusteringe winde,
    when greater trees doe crashe.   32
The lowe and meane estate
    is surest thinge, I finde;
The Courtlie life vnstedfast is,
    more fleeting than the winde.   36
There spend they all they haue,
    and more, if need require;
They gape for this, they watch for that,
    they followe ech desire.   40
They frowne vpon their frends,
    and fawne vpon there foes;
They envie all the favored,
    they scorne the mann in woes;   44

They presse vpon the prince,
   they glose for hope of gayne;
[leaf 67] they hate the wise, they ride the fooles,
   they laughe and loue in vaine.   48
They seeke with greatest shewe
   for to maintaine their route;
They pinche and spare, they carke and muse,
   to bringe the same about.   52
Thus, vnder all this shewe
   and troope of goulden sights,
They doe possesse vnrestfull daies
   and thowsand woefull nights.   56
ffore loe, this goulden miserie,
   as I doe finde, is naught,
But highe disdaine Ioynd with distresse
   and manie mourning thought.   60
Wheras my Cuntrye life,
   which nowe I take in hand,
Bringes quiet rest, a carelesse minde,
   it needes noe lustie band.   64
Wee envie noe estate,
   wee loue the porest sorte;
We lavishe not Ill gotten goods,
   wee keepe a meaner port.   68
Wee spend as reason bidds,
   wee entertaine our frend
[leaf 67, back] In honnest state; and when you lack,
   then must wee seeme to lend;   72
which is farr better case,
   at neede allwaies to haue,
Then for to spend without a reine,
   and then haue need to craue.   76
Our garments are not gaye,
   our garners haue the more;
wee seeke noe statelie halls, nor hante
   the Princes Court therfore,   80

But live in pore estate,
  more quiet in our brest
Then those whome dailie service doth
  procure soe much vnrest. 84
Wee passe the silent night
  with his vnbroken sleepe;
Wee ease our heavie minde with mirth;
  of loue wee take noe keepe. 88
I therfore flie the presse
  and troope of Courtlie trayne
And scorne their pride that scorne my fall,
  to rest from restles payne. 92
I leaue the Courtlie life
  to those that skillesse are,
And hedlonge runn by others harms,   [leaf e8]
  that soone will not beware. 96
My cottage doth content
  my well contented minde;
My wantoun yowth is gone, and nowe
  grave thoughts in hedd I finde. 100
Thus well I tried haue,
  that my mishappe hath wrought,
More quiet state for my behoofe
  then I had ever thoughte. 104
In happie tyme, therefore,
  I banishd such a life,
where no thinge certaine maie be found,
  where all things are but strife. 108
Thus, carefull Court, farwell!
  and wellcome Cuntrie state,
where thow shalt live at quiet rest
  from all envyenge hate. 112

(72) The number 1, 2, 3, 4.

One simple thinge cann nothinge worke,
    yt maie not stand, but fall.
Twoe maie both much and great things doe;
    but three maie compasse all.   4

[leaf 68, back] And fower, I trulie finde to bee
    perfection of ech thinge,
ffor in the same conteyned is
    what heaven and earth maye bringe.   8

Woe, then, to him that is alone,
    Kinge *Dauids* sonne cold saye,
for yf he fall, he wanteth helpe
    to raise him or to staye.   12

But where twoe things doe meete in one,
    as nature help'd by art,
There mann maye prove miraculous,
    through his celestiall part.   16

But rightlie yf these worthie two
    themselves from Center spred
To three kinds of Philosophie,
    newe Creatures maie be bred.   20

ffor if divine Philosophie,
    the naturall and morrall,
ffrom Center spred themselves abrode
    and then in Center fall,   24

There wilbe vnion of these three,
    Sol, lune, and *Mercurie;*
ffor in the heaven and Earth three things
    the truth do testifie: 28

[leaf 69] All which Saint Iohn did trulie knowe,
    and therefore rightlie tould
That three is one, and one is three,
    which fewe menn cann vnfould.   32

But if with all this secrett three
    the number fower be placed,
In *Tetragramaton* I finde
    the worke shall well be graced.   36
Add therefore one to three and fower,[1]   [1 ? to 2, 3, 4 = 9]
    makinge the number tenn,
In w*hi*ch enclosed is the skill
    fast lock'd from common menn.   40
Take this my sweete conceyt in worth,
    though worthlesse vnto thee,
whose sacred witt, with abstruse skill
    is fraught in ech degree.   44

---

(73) [2]Mr Camdens Britania.

[2 ? MS. K or another letter I can't read.]

The holie licor (whose mysteries divine   1
to *Venus* Squire consecrate are seene)
needes not the Poets braunch (touchstone of wyne),
the Clyming Ivye allwaies freshe and greene,   4
In Sommers scorchinge heate and winters could,
to make that wyne the better to be sould.   6

And learned *Camden*, with his searching witt, 7 [leaf 69, back]
whose deepe studie, by travells carefull payne,
hath from errors and mace[3] of *Dedalus* pitt,   [3 maze]
(for Cuntries loue,) drawne vnto light agayne   10
worthye Antiquities, wherof before
none sayed the like, or shall doe anie more.   12

This *Philopolites* needeth not, I saye,   13
My rough pensill to portrait his desart;
but as good wyne commends it self allwaie
without the Ivye signe, soe in noe part   16
he needes noe prayse, synce that his learned quill
with flowing style his prayses doth distill.   18

ffor by his guide the *Roman* names doe live,   19
and ancient things consum'd by cancred byte

of ould Iniurious tyme, he doth revive,
in *Latiane* tongue, a worke w*hi*ch breedes delight 22
and Cuntries good, to such as will embrace
soe rare a gemm not found in other place. 24

His deepe conceit I highlie doe admire, 25
his strange Invention I knowe not howe to praise,
the truth of things whereto he doth aspire
is past my reach to shewe by anie waies; 28
[leaf 70] what will you more? breifelie, this thing I teach,
hee hath donne that w*hi*ch noe mann ells could reach.

Buy then this worke! doe read and reade againe! 31
esteeme the mann, as hee doth merrit well!
requite w*i*th thanks the frute of Endlesse payne
represse envye! in vaine! since I knowe well, 34
to seeke a knott in rushe thow maist contend,
and teare w*i*th spite what thow canst not amende. 36

(74) Solomons witt.

ffreind *Eldrington*, thow art as wise
    As *Salomon*, menn saye,
ffor thow art like to him in witt,
    in earnest and in playe. 4

But what is like, is not the same,
    as all menn well doe finde:
Soe thow hast not *Solomons* witt
    in all points of his minde. 8

Yet in one thinge thow dost the height
    of his rare witt expresse,
In chaunge of *Venus* sweete delights
    and Lecheries excesse. 12

[leaf 70, back] In other thinges thow art not hee,
    noe more then is an Ape,
Whoe is like thee in Peevishe witt
    and in deformed shape. 16

Thus must I playe with thy fyne witt,
   to answere thy fonde Ieste,
That scoffes at everie meaner witt,
   which wisemenn doe detest. 20

(75) Leylandes rightefull ghost.

What *Endore* phytonesse, what envious hart, 1
what fourth furie, what rage of witlesse braine
Doth vex my sprite against his due desart,
and force me causelesse, wronglie to complaine? 4
one guiltlesse hand, which doth mye fame retaine,
all thoughe detractinge penn with deepe despite
cannot behould the beames of Englands lighte. 7

My name, my fame, my labors, and my penn, 8
my indigested worke of highe conceit,
came not to be obscur'd in thanklesse *Denne*,
ffor he (whome skillesse malice through deceit 11
sekes to entrapp with hooke of scorning beyt)
doth gratefullie receyve my buryed name,
which otherwise had perished to my shame. 14

By him I live, by him the world doth knowe, 15
by him the heauens and humane Lawes doe finde
that he hath, farr beyond my broken shewe,
his Cuntries glorie in one worke combinde, 18
with gratious style, and sprite of heavenlie minde,
which both to mine and his immortall praise,
in spite of spite, will honnored bee allwaies. 21

And therefore, in most humble sort, doe sue 22
that Learn'd *Camden* his right guerdon maye haue,
and that those coniuringe words maie finde ther due,
which vex my sprite, and raise me from my grave, 25
whoe never deem'd his learning to deprave
ffor I confesse, he rarelie doth compleate
that famous worke which I could not entreate. 28

(76) Quiet and Rest.

As wearie bodie doth restore his strength w*it*h rest,
as fertill soyle sometimes vntild doth prove the best,
As laboringe beastes, the ox, the horse, must quiet haue,
as toylinge daie, the restefull night doth dulie crave, 4

[leaf 71, back] As bowe still bent, in time is weake
  and looseth strength,
As Sommers flowers in Winters rootes
  doe reste at length,—   8
Soe must the rulinge minde, the seate
  where reasone reynes,
with quiet recreate it self
  from former paynes.   12
ffor what wants interchanged rest
  will weare awaye,
And restles paines, both witt and wealth,
  doth soone decaye.   16
Then cease, thow wearie muse, allwaies
  to beate thy brayne
And weare thy paynefull hand,
  w*hi*ch never reaped gaine;   20
Since all thy sweating toyle finds but
  such hard event
As damned *Sisiphus*,
  most bitter punishement,   24
Wherbye thy goulden tyme
  thow thriftelesse dost consume,
Like *Gebers Cooke*, to waste thy wealth
  in Ayerye fume.   28
         Finis.

NOTES.

p. 2. *Chyrill.* "He (Lysander) always kept the Spartan poet Choerilus in his retinue, that he might be ready to add lustre to his actions by the powers of verse. And when Antilochus had written some stanzas in his praise, he was so delighted that he gave him his hat full of silver." Lysander, Langhorne's *Plutarch.*—S. See note on p. 77, l. 13, p. 104.

p. 6, l. 4. *Genius.* A Roman kept holiday and sacrificed to his genius or guardian spirit on important occasions such as birthdays. Hence the phrase "indulgere genio," to enjoy oneself.—S.

p. 7 (3), l. 6. *Ceres.* "It is an old and well-known sentence, 'Sine Cerere et Baccho friget Venus' (love grows cool without bread and wine)." Burton's *Anatomy of Melancholy.* Love Melancholy, Numb. V., Subsect. 1.—S.

p. 16, l. 8. *Basiliske.* "To come now unto the Basiliske, whom all other serpents do flie from and are affraid of: albeit he killeth them with his very breath and smel that passeth from him; yea, and (by report) if he do but set his eie on a man it is enough to take away his life."—Holland's *Pliny,* tom. II., p. 356, ed. 1635. "bred it is in the province Cyrenaica, and is not above twelve fingers bredth long: a white spot like a starre it carrieth on the head, and sets it out like a coronet or diadem: if he but hisse once, no other serpents dare come neere: hee creepeth not winding and crawling byas as other serpents doe, with one part of the body driving, the other forward, but goeth upright and aloft from the ground with one halfe part of his body: he killeth all trees and shrubs not onely that he toucheth, but also that hee breatheth upon: as for grasse and herbes, those he sindgeth and burneth up, yea, and breaketh stones in sunder; so venimous and deadly he is. It is received for a truth, that one of them on a time was killed with a launce by an horsman from his horse-back, but the poison was so strong that went from his body along the staffe, as it killed both horse and man: and yet a silly weazle hath a deadly power to kill this monstrous serpent, as pernicious as it is [for many kings have been desirous to see the experience thereof, and the manner how he is killed]. See how Nature hath delighted to match every thing in the world with a concurrent. The manner is, to cast these weazles into the hole and cranies where they lye, (and easie they be to know by the stinking sent of the place about them :) they are not so soone within, but they overcome them with their strong smell, but they die themselves withall;

and so Nature for her pleasure hath the combat dispatched." *Ibid.* tom. I., p. 206-7.—S.

p. 23, No. 25, l. 1. *The Melitane Dogge.* "A Melitean Dog, or a little Dog for a Ladies Lap."—*Minshue,* 1626.

"A little pretty dog which women use to play with: a Fisting[1] hound. *Melitæus canis.*"—*Gouldman's Lat. Dict.,* 1669.

"An animal once peculiar to *Malta,* is the small dog with a long silken coat, mentioned by Pliny, which Buffon calls *bichon;* but this race of dogs is now extinct."—*Penny Cyclopædia.*

"The little dogs and all,
Tray, Blanch, and Sweet-heart, see, they bark at me."—*Lear,* III. 6.

. . . . . "as full of quarrel and offence
As my young mistress' dog."—*Othello,* II. 3.

Probably the dogs referred to in the above two passages may have been of the Maltese breed; as also may have been the "Jewel" Proteus sent to Sylvia, and which was stolen from Launce by the hangman-boys.—P. A. DANIEL.

Strabo of the Melitæan Dogs. "There is a Town in *Pachynus,* a Promontory of *Sicily* (called *Melita*[2]), from whence are transported many fine little Dogs called, *Melitæi Canes;* they were accounted the Jewels[3] of Women; but now [A.D. 1607] the said Town is possessed by Fishermen, and there is no such reckoning made of those tender little Dogs,—for these are not bigger then common Ferrets, or Weasils,—yet are they not small in understanding, nor mutable in their love to men: for which cause they are also nourished tenderly for pleasure; whereupon came the proverb, *Militæa Catella,* for one nourished for pleasure; and *Canis digna throno,* because Princes hold them in their hands, sitting upon their estate.[4]

Ælianus. "Theodorus, the tumbler and dancer, had one of these, which loved him so well, that at his death he leaped into the fire after *Blondus.* his body. Now a dayes, they have found another breed of little Dogs in all Nations, beside the *Melitæan* Dogs, either made so by *The art of making of little Dogs.* art, as inclosing their bodies in the earth when they are Whelps,—so as they cannot grow great, by reason of the place,—or else, lessening and impayring their growth, by some kind of meat or nourishment. These are called in *Germany,*

---

[1] ? One to be handled. But the term may be susceptible of a less cleanly interpretation. See the extract on page 100—"*which some frumpingly term Fysting Hound.*"—P. A. D.

[2] Melita is no doubt Malta, the island south of Pachynus.

[3] Compare Proteus in *The Two Gentlemen of Verona,* IV. iv., "*Launce.* Marry, Sir, I carried mistress Silvia the dog you bade me. *Pro.* And what says she to my little *jewel?*"

[4] See, in Shaw's "Dresses and Decorations of the Middle Ages," Vol. 2, the portrait of Constancia Duchess of Lancaster, wife of John of Gaunt, with one of these little dogs in her lap: from an Illuminated MS. in the Brit. Museum, date about 1525.—P. A. D.

Bracken Schosshundle and *Gutschenhundle;* the *Italians, Bottolo*[1]*;* other Nations have no common name for this kind that I know. Martial made this Distichon of a little French Dog; for about *Lions* in *France* there are store of this kinde, and are sold very dear; sometimes for ten Crowns, and sometimes for more.

Delicias parvæ si vis audire catellæ,
Narranti brevis est pagina tota mihi.

They are not above a foot, or half a foot long; and alway the lesser the more delicate and precious. Their head like the head of a Mouse, but greater, their snowt sharp, their ears like the ears of a Cony, short legs, little feet, long tail, and white colour, and the hairs about the shoulders longer then ordinary, is most commended. They are of pleasant disposition, and will leap and bite without pinching, and bark prettily; and some of them are taught to stand upright, holding up their fore legs like hands; other to fetch and carry in their mouths, that which is cast unto them.

"There be some wanton women which admit them to their beds, and bring up their young ones in their own bosomes, for they are so tender, that they seldom bring above one at a time, but they lose their life. It was reported that when *Grego* in *Syracuse* was to go from home among other Gossips, she gave her maid charge of two things: one, that she should look to her childe when it cryed; the other, that she should keep the little Dog within doors."—Topsell's *Hist. of Four-footed Beasts* (1607), p. 128, ed. 1658.

Ib. p. 135; from "the Treatise of English Dogs, first of all written in *Latin* by that famous Doctor in Physick *John Cay*[2], and since translated by A[braham] F[leming]," printed in 1576, blk. lr., 4to., 30 leaves.

"Of the delicate, neat, and prety kind of *DOGS* called the *SPANIEL GENTLE, or the COMFORTER;* in Latin, *Melitæus,* or *Fotor.*

"There is, besides those which we have already delivered, another sort of Gentle Dogs in this our *English* soil, but exempted from the order of the residue: the Dogs of this kind doth *Callimachus* call *Melitæos,* of the Island *Melita,* in the sea of Sicily (which at this day is named *Malta*) an Island indeed, famous and renowned with couragious and puissant Souldiers, valiantly fighting under the banner of Christ their unconquerable Captain) where this kind of Dogs had their principal beginning. These dogs are little, prety, proper, and fine, and sought for to satisfie the delicateness of dainty dames and wanton

---

[1] *Bottolo,* a whelpe, a puppie, a sheapheards cur, a filthie dog. Also as *Bottarissa* [a kinde of lampreie or eele-poute].—*Florio,* 1598. *Faldarello,* a little prettie dogge, a playing dogge, a puppie sitting vpon a womans cotes.—*Ib.*

[2] Dr John Caius, born 6 Oct. 1510, at Norwich, died 29 July 1573. Physician to Edw. VI., Mary, and Elizabeth. Gonville Hall, Cambridge, enlarged by him, now known as Caius College. His real name was Kaye or Key, which he latinized. Supposed by some, without much probability, to be the Dr Caius of the "Merry Wives of Windsor."—P. A. D.

womens wils, instruments of folly for them to play and dally withal, to trifle away the treasure of time, to withdraw their mindes from more commendable exercises, and to content their corrupted concupiscences with vain disport (a silly shift to shun irksome idleness). These puppies, the smaller they be, the more pleasure they provoke, as more meet playfellowes for minsing mistresses to bear in their bosomes, to keep company withal in their Chambers, to succour with sleep in bed, and nourish with meat at bord, to lay in their laps, and lick their lips as they ride in their Waggons : and good reason it should be so, for courseness with fineness hath no fellowship, but featness with neatness hath neighbourhood enough. That plausible proverb verified upon a Tyrant, namely, that he loved his Sow better then his Son, may well be applyed to these kind of people, who delight more in Dogs that are deprived of all possibility of reason, then they do in children that be Capeable of wisdom and judgement. But this abuse peradventure reigneth where there hath been long lack of issue, or else where barrenness is the best blossom of beauty."—*Ib.* p. 135.

(Page 140.) "A start to *out-landish DOGS* in this conclusion, not impertinent to the Authors purpose.

"Use and custome hath entertained other Dogs of an Out-landish kind, but a few, and the same being of a pretty bigness, I mean Island[1] Dogs, curled and rough all over, which by reason of the length of their hair, make shew neither of face nor of body : And yet these Curs, forsooth, because they are so strange, are greatly set by, esteemed, taken up, and many times in the room of the Spaniel gentle or comforter. The nature of men is so moved, nay, rather maryed to novelties without all reason, wit, judgement, or perseverance, *Eromen allotrias*, paroromen suggeneis

> *Out-landish toys we take with delight,*
> *Things of our own Nation we have in despight.*

Which fault remaineth not in us concerning Dogs only, but for Artificers also. And why ? it is manifest that we disdain and contemn our own Work-men, be they never so skilful, be they never so cunning, be they never so excellent. A beggerly Beast brought out of barbarous borders, from the uttermost Countreys Northward, &c., we stare at, we gaze at, we muse, we marvail at, like an Ass of *Cumanum*, like *Thales* with the brazen shanks, like the man in the Moon.

[1] Iceland dogs, like our Skye terriers now.—F. "*Pistol.* Pish for thee, Iceland dog ! thou prick-ear'd cur of Iceland ! (*Island* Ff. *Iseland* Qq.)— *Henry V.*, II. i. 44. See notes on this passage in Var. ed. 1821."—P. A. D.
Sir O. Smallshanks [to his intended]:
> You shall have jewels,
> A baboon, a parrot, and an *Iceland dog.—Ram Alley*, iii. 1.
> —would I might be
> Like a dog under her table, and serve for a footstool,
> So I might have my belly full of that
> Her *Island cur* refuses.—Massinger, *Ph. Picture*, V. 1.

"The which default *Hippocrates* marked when he was alive, as evidently appeareth in the beginning of his Book *Peri Agmon*, so entituled and named.

"And we in our work entituled *De Ephemera Britannica*,[1] to the people of *England* have more plentifully expressed. In this kinde, look which is most blockish, and yet most waspish, the same is most esteemed; and not among Citizens only, and jolly Gentlemen, but among lusty Lords also, and Noblemen."

(Page 142, Jn. Cay, transl. by Abr. Fleming). "Now leaving the surview of hunting and hawking Dogs, it remaineth that we run over the residue, whereof some be called fine Dogs, some course, other some, Mungrels or Rascals. The first is Spaniel gentle, called *Canis Melitœus*, because it is a kinde of dog accepted among Gentils, Nobles, Lords, Ladies, &c., who make much of them, vouchsafing to admit them so far into their company, that they will not only lull them in their laps, but kiss them with their lips, and make them their pretty play-fellows. Such a one was Gorgons little puppy mentioned by *Theocritus* in *Syracuse*, who, taking his journey, straightly charged and commanded his Maid to see to his Dog as charily and warily as to his childe: To call him in always, that he wandred not abroad, as well as to rock the babe asleep, crying in the Cradle. This Pupperly and pleasant Cur, (which some frumpingly tearm Fysting Hound) serves in a manner to no good use, except (as we have made former relation) to succour and strengthen qualing and qualming stomachs, to bewray bawdery, and filthy abhominable lewdness (which a little Dog of this kinde did in *Sicilia*) as *Ælianus* in his 7 Book of Beasts, and 27 Chapter, recordeth." p. 142.

p. 26, l. 15. *Medusas slater*. When Perseus cut off the head of the Gorgon Medusa, Pegasus sprang from the headless trunk.—S.

p. 27. *Revenge*. "Also an hound is wrathfull and malicious, so that for to awreak himselfe, he biteth oft the stone that is throwen to him; and biteth the stone with great madnesse, that he breaketh his own teeth, and grieueth not the stone, but his owne teeth full sore." 1582. *Batman vppon Bartholome, his Booke* De Proprietatibus Rerum, *Newly corrected*, &c., leaf 355, back, col. 2.

p. 27. *Revenge*. "Where-in they resemble angry Dogges, which byte the stone, not him that throweth it." Lyly's *Euphues*, p. 223, Arber's ed.—S.

p. 28, l. 16. *the fruitfull horne*. The horn of the goat Amaltheia who suckled the infant Zeus, called cornucopia, the horn of plenty.—S.

p. 28 (32), l. 19. *Halcyon daies*. "This very bird so notable is little bigger than a sparrow: for the more part of her pennage, blew, intermingled yet among with white and purple feathers, having a thin smal neck and long withall.—It is a very great chance to see one of these Halcyones, & never are they seen but about the setting of the star Virgiliæ, [i. the Broodhen] or els neere Mid-summer or Mid-winter:

[1] This work ought to be Englisht and reprinted.

for otherwhiles they will flie about a ship, but soone are they gone again and hidden. They lay and sit about Mid-winter when daies be shortest : & the time whiles they are broody, is called the Halcyon daies, for during that season the sea is calme and navigable, especially in the coast of Sicilie." Holland's *Pliny*, tom. I., p. 287.—S.

p. 29, l. 1. *Remora*. "¶ Also, kinde of fish hath diuersitie of shape, and of disposition, both in quality & in quantitie. For there is some kinde of great huge fish, with great bodies & huge, as it were mountaines and hills, as Isi[dore] saith : such was the whale that swallowed *Ionas* the Prophet ; his wombe was so great that it might be called hell : for the Prophet saith : ' In that wombe of hell he heard me.' And ther be some fish so small, & *that* vnneth they be taken with hooks, as Isi[dore] saith .li. 12. *Afforus* is a little fish ; & for littleness, it may not be taken with hooks : and there it is said *that* *Enchirius* is a fish vnneth halfe a foote long, and hath that name, of *Herendo*, cleauing : for though he be full little of body, nevertheles he is most of vertue : for he cleaueth to *the* ship, & holdeth it still steadfastly in the sea, as though the ship were on grounde therein. Though windes blowe, and waues arise strongly, and woode stormes, that ships may not mooue neyther passe. And that Fish holdeth not still the shippe by any craft, but onely by cleauing to *the* ship. Latines call this fish *Moron*. For by strength he maketh the ship to stand, as it is said.

" (*Addition*. As touching this strange fish, whose smalnesse, with his vertue of staieng ships, doth passe mans reason : the Grecians cal *Ethneis*, of the Latines *Remora*, because she doth stay ships. *Opianus* and *Aelian* write, that he delighteth most in *the* high seas : he is of length a cubit, that is, halfe a yard, of a browne conlour, like vnto an Eele : diuerse opinions are of this fish, but all authours agree *that*, for a manifest truth, such a kind ther is, whereof one of these Fishes stayed the Galley of *Caius Cæsar*. *Plinie* meruailing, sayth : ' Oh straunge and wonderfull thing ! that, all the windes blowing, and the most furious tempests raging, notwithstanding the violence of the same, yet doth this small Fish holde steadie the ship whereto he is fastened, so greate is the secrete of nature, by the ordinaunce of God.' Moreouer, by trauailing the coastes of *America*, the later trauailers reporte to haue felt the strength and vertue of the same kinde of fish.)"—1582. Batman vppon Bartholome, his Booke *De Proprietatibus Rerum*, lf. 199, col. 2.

p. 29, (33), l. 1. *Remora*. " But to returne again unto our Stay-Ship Echeneis : Trebius Niger saith it is a foot long, and five fingers thicke, and that oftentimes it stayeth a ship." Holland's *Pliny*, tom. I., p. 249. Pliny says that it stopped Caligula's galley once who " fumed and fared as an Emperour taking great indignation that so small a thing as it should hold him back perforce—notwithstanding there were no fewer than foure hundred lusty men in his galley that laboured at the ore all that ever they could to the contrary—it resembled for all the world a snaile of the greatest making." *Ib*. tom. II., p. 426.—S.

p. 30 (36), l. 9. *Terminus.* " When the temple of Jupiter was to be built on the Capitoline hill, the other deities allowed their shrines to be removed to make room, but Terminus the boundary god refused to yield." Ovid, *Fasti,* II., 667-70.—S.

p. 33 (40), l. 17. Rev. xxi. 27.—S.

p. 39, l. 6. *Crane carrying a stone in its bill.* Mr P. A. Daniel refers to Lyly's *Euphues,* p. 216, 416, of Arber's reprint. " What I haue done, was onely to keep my selfe from sleepe, as the Crane doth the stone in hir foote; and I would also, with the same Crane, I had been silent, *holding a stone in my mouth."*—p. 216. " The tongue of a louer should be like the poynt in the Diall, which, though it go, none can see it going, or a young tree, which, though it growe, none can see it growing; hauing alwayes *the stone in their mouth which the Cranes vse when they flye ouer mountaines, least they make a noyse."*—p. 416.

p. 40 (52), l. 1. Daulis in Phocis was the scene of the murder of Itys, for which crime Philomela was turned into a nightingale.—S.

p. 41 (53), l. 8. " Bellerophon tried to ascend to heaven on the back of Pegasus, but the winged horse threw him." *Pind. Isth.* 6.—S.

p. 47. *Mr Thomas Valence,* one of the Lincoln's-Inn friends of Lord Chancellor Egerton and Francis Thynne. Mr Martin Doyle, the Steward of Lincoln's Inn, has kindly searcht the entry-books of the Inn for me, and says: " I find the name of 'Thomas Vallence' (so spelt) as admitted of the Society on the 4th of March, 2 Eliz. [A.D. 1560]. The entry is on p. 256 of the Black Book No. 4. His manucaptors were Thomas Wotton and Thomas Morgan.

" In the Admission Book No. 1, on p. 4, and again on p. 45, there is the signature of 'Thomas Valence' written with one *l* only."

In Stow's Survey of London (ed. Strype), vol. i., p. 734, under the heading *Monuments,* in the Parish Church of St Dunstan's in the West, is

" In obitum Thomæ Valentis, Lincolniensis Hospitii Socii. Qui obiit 23 die Decemb. Anno 1601, ætatis 78.

<small>A small monument in the east end of the Chancel, north.</small>
Hoc tumulo Thomæ requiescunt ossa Valentis,
Et parvum corpus parvula terra tegit:
Sed mens, quæ melior pars est, expersque sepulchri,
Infima despiciens, sidera celsa colit."

Colonel Chester—my kind helper about Wm Thynne's will, &c.—adds: " This monument also called Valence 'Esquire,' and gave his arms, *viz.* Chequy or and sable, on a chief gules 3 leopards faces fleure or. According to the parish register of St Dunstan, he died at his rooms in Lincoln's Inn, ' lying over the gate.'

" I may add that he was the author of some Latin verses prefixed to Cooper's *Thesaurus,* fol. 1573.

" I have his will—that of Thomas Valence, of Lincoln's Inn, Esq.—dated 14th Sep. 1600, and proved 31 Dec. 1601, by his ' loving good Cousin ' John Williams, Fellow of All Souls College, Oxford, and his 'trusty servant' James Marshall of Furnival's Inn, Gent. The only bequest in it is one of 20s. to his servant Allan Gilpin; but he explains that he had the same day disposed of his estate by a deed of gift, and cites the Indenture tripartite, as between him of the 1st part, his said executors of the 2nd part, and Percival Willoughby of Middleton, co. Warwick, John Southcott of Bulwer, co. Essex, Thomas Denne of Adesham, co. Kent, and Richard Carey of London, Esq., of the 3rd part ; and he intimates that his estate is to be disposed of according to the directions therein.

"This Indenture will probably be found among the Rolls in Chancery."

p. 48, l. 15. In the lesser triumph called an ovation the successful general wore the *Corona ovalis*, a crown of myrtle instead of the laurel wreath. There seems to be no authority for an olive crown, but the olive branch was a symbol of peace.—S.

p. 53 (1), l. 1. For the lion as the symbol of Judah, see Gen. xlix. 9.—S.

p. 53 (1), l. 6. The lions in the royal arms and the fleur de lys.—S.

p. 58, l. 17. *trust Ovid*. Thynne perhaps refers to *Art. Amat.* III., 653-6.—S.

p. 62, l. 9. Chaucer's *Hous of Fame*.

" But as I slept, me mette I was
Withyn a temple ymade of glas."—S.

p. 62, l. 11. *a glasse in verse*. A satire on contemporary manners, &c., entitled the Steele Glas, published 1576, written by George Gascoigne, ob. 1577.—S.

p. 67 (32), l. 1. "Of all places they [criminals] hold Holborne hill an unfortunate place to ride up. It seems they goe that way unwillingly, for they are drawne. They cannot misse their way to their Journeys end, they are so guarded and guided."—London and the Countrey Carbonadoed and Quartred into severall Characters, by D. Lupton, 1632.—S.

p. 70 (37). A free translation of an epigram by Sir Thomas More, which will be found in Cayley's *Memoirs of Sir Thomas More*, vol. II., p. 325. Thynne has added the retort of the discourteous knight.—S.

p. 72 (42), l. 3. *carding*, playing at cards. Compare the possible sense of 'carded' in 1 *Hen. IV.*, III. ii. 62, "carded his state," and Ritson's note thereon:—"*By carding his state*, the king means that his predecessor set his consequence to hazard, played it away (as a man loses his fortune) at *cards*." This is a much disputed passage ; see notes in Variorum Sh., ed. 1821.—P. A. D.

p. 77, l. 13. *Cherill.* "*Cherillus*, one no very good Poet, had for every verse well made, a Phillips noble of gold," etc.—Puttenham, Arber's reprint, p. 32.—P. A. D.

'Cherilus, who wrote a poem on the victory of the Athenians over Xerxes, and on the exploits of Alexander the Great. Only 7 of his verses were approved ; and for these he received 7 pieces of gold: for every other verse, a buffet.'—B. N.

p. 77, l. 16. *Gouldings learned rewe.* Arthur Golding, a contemporary of Thynne, translated Ovid's *Metamorphoses*, &c., &c., into English. Puttenham (*The Arte of English Poesie*, Arber's ed., p. 75), after mentioning Dr Phaer's Virgil, says, "Since him followed Maister Arthure Golding, who with no lesse commendation turned into English meetre the Metamorphosis of Ovide."

Webbe (*Discourse of English Poetrie*, Arber's ed., p. 51), after criticizing Phaer's Virgil, says, "Master Golding—hath equally deserved commendations for the beautifying of the English speeche."—S.

p. 80, ll. 11—14. The Apostles creed is divided into twelve articles. The youth perhaps means: One twelfth of my creed I have ceased to believe in, He descended into Hell, for if Christ never saw London he never saw hell.—S.

p. 81 (60), l. 7. *Francis George.* A Venetian, the author of a book entitled *Problemata in Sacram Scripturam*, Paris, 1574, the work probably referred to here.

"A Venetian monk, Francis Georgius, published a scheme of blended Cabbalistic and Platonic, or Neo-Platonic philosophy, in 1525." *Hallam's Literature of Europe.*—S.

p. 82 (61), l. 15. *oten ryme.* Pastoral poetry. *Avena*, an oaten straw, was used poetically for the shepherd's reed pipe.—S.

p. 85, l. 43. *Pittacus.* One of the seven wise men of Greece. The maxim is first found in Theognis.—S.

p. 86 (67), l. 6. The *tria verba* were the three words used by the Roman prætor in a civil action, *Do, Dico, Addico,* the first in granting permission to try the case, the second in giving judgment, the third in assigning the disputed property to one of the litigants. Their application here is not very obvious, but perhaps the gentleman satirized was wont to lay down the law upon all matters under discussion with the solemnity of a Judge.—S.

p. 88 (71). *The Courte and Cuntrey.* Compare the interesting tracts reprinted by Mr W. C. Hazlitt in his Roxburghe-Library *Inedited Tracts*, 1868:—1. 'The English Courtier and the Countreygentleman: A pleasant and learned Disputation betweene them both: very profitable and necessarie to be read of all Nobilitie and Gentlemen. Wherein is discoursed, what order of lyfe best beseemeth a Gentleman, (as well for education, as the course of his whole life) to make him a person fytte for the publique seruice of his Prince and Countrey'. London, Richard Iones, 1586;—

2. Nicholas Breton's 'The Court and Country, or A Briefe Discourse betweene the Courtier and Country-man; of the Manner, Nature, and Condition of their liues. Dialogue-wise set downe betwixt a Courtier and Country-man. Conteyning many Delectable and Pithy Sayings, worthy Observation. Also, necessary Notes for a Courtier'. London, G. Eld. 1618.

p. 92, l. 9. Ecclesiastes iv. 10.—S.

p. 93, l. 3, 4. *Ivye.* 'Good wine needs no bush.' The 'Ivy-bush' was—I believe is still—the sign of many a tavern.—P. A. D.

p. 95 (75). In 1594 Ralph Brook, or Brooksmouth, York Herald, published a book entitled, "A Discoverie of certain errors published in print in the much commended Britannia,' in which, besides pointing out errors in the Britannia, he asserted that Camden had obtained much of his material from Leland. Leland had been commissioned by Henry VIII. to make collections for a history and topography of England and Wales, but at his death his unpublished MSS. were dispersed. Thynne here admits that Camden was indebted to these MSS., but urges that by his use of them he rescued Leland's work from oblivion.

"This *Ralph Brooksmouth* as he had wrote a very virulent Book against *Camden*, entitled, *A Discovery of Errors*, and endeavouring therein to charge his *Britannia* with many Errors, especially in Matters of Genealogy and Heraldry; and that since Queen *Elizabeth* had made him *Clarentieux:* So *Camden* modestly, but learnedly, answered that angry Man, and vindicated what he had writ; and set his Answer at the End of an Edition of his *Britannia, Anno* .1600. This *Herald* wrote yet another Piece against *Clarencieux*, pretending to a Second Discovery of Errors in his *Britannia*, and in Justification of what he had published before; and that he had stolen from *Leland:* Therein he hath these Words, (the very MS. was very obligingly shewn me by *John Anstis*, Esq; *Garter* King at Arms) viz.:

"His new coated *Britannia*, made and digested of industrious Labours of *John Leyland*, that great Scholar, and painful Searcher of *England's* Antiquities,—as may appear both by the said *Leylands* Six Volumes, written with his own Hand, yet extant in Custody of Mr *Osborne* of the *Exchequer;* as also by the said *Leyland's New-Year's Gift*, dedicated to the same King, annexed to the End of my late *Discovery:* Which Six Books or Volumes were copied out by *John Stow*, and by him sold to this *Learned Man* [*Camden*] for an Annuity of Eight Pounds *per Annum;* which he did pay unto the said *Stowe*, during his Life; as the said *John Stowe* himself, before his Death, confessed to divers Persons of Credit; lamenting the Wrong done to *Leyland*, both by that Learned Man; and also by one *Harrison* of *Wyndesore*, who likewise had robbed *Leyland* of the Islands adjacent to this Realm of *England;* setting them in *Hollingshed*, as his own Travels and Collection, &c. These Lines, reflecting unworthily upon *Stow*, as well as *Camden*, are easily answered; since both do freely acknowledge when they have made use of *Leyland*, by setting his Name in their Margins."

Life of Stow by Strype, prefixed to his edition of Stowe's Survey, p. x—xi.—S.

p. 96, l. 27. "Geber, a native of Harran in Mesopotamia, lived in the 9th century. He wrote several works on the philosopher's stone." D'Herbelot, sub voce *Giaber.*—S.

INDEX.

8/22 means 'page 8, l. 22'; 64 (27) 1 means 'p. 64, poem 27, l. 1.'

Acheron, 8/22.
Acteons curres, 45/23.
Actius, 2.
Adame, 81 (60), 10.
Adrian, 11/5.
Aetna monte, 66/13.
Aglaia, 14 (13), 13.
Alciat, 3.
Alderman woodcock, 74 (46), 4. The woodcock seems to have been a type of folly. Bewick says that it is easily caught in snares. "O this *woodcock*, what an ass it is."— *Taming of the Shrew*, I. ii. 161.
Amalthea, 28/15; 101.
Amicla, 17/9.
Androgenon, 82 (60), 15.
annoyance, 22 (23), 8, harm.
Antiochus, 2.
Antipater, 86 (67), 13.
Antomedon, 64 (27), 1, Automedon.
Apollo, 30 (35), 9; 37/7; 88 (70), 2, 12, 19.
Arionian dolphins, 50/16.
Aschainus, 5/9, Ascanius.
asured, 38/7, azure.
Athens, 3.

Bacchus, 17 (15), 6, 10, 11, 13, 17, 26; 27 (30), 3; 28 (32), 18.
Bacchus juice, 60 (15), 7, wine.
Bacchus plant, 82 (61), 1, ivy.

basiliske, the, 16/8, 16; 97.
bat, 46 (60), 6. "A Batte, baculum."—Levins, *Man. Voc.*, E. E. T. S.
bate, *sb.* 84/8, debate.
Bavius, 1.
Bayarde, 1.
be, 18/27, by.
bedds, *v. n.* 19 (18), 14.
beforne, 27 (30), 6, before.
Bellepheron, 26 (28), 8, 13, Bellerephon, 41 (53), 1; 103.
Bellerus, 25 (28), 4, Beller, 26 (28), 7.
Bellona, 28/9.
bliste, *p. p.* 86 (67), 3, blest.
blood of earth, 60 (15), 9, water.
boghed, *adj.* 1.
borde, *sb.* 55/16, the table.
bould, be, 88/15, be sure.
bowe, *sb.* 16/20, bough?
bragg, *sb.* 22 (22), 7.
brain sick witts, 14 (12), 20.
brickle, *adj.* 18/2, brittle.
Brooksmouth, Ralph, 106.
Browne, 62 (20), 1.
but to, 53/10, save, except.
Byas, 11/7.

Cambridge, 57 (8), 2.
Camden, 93/7; 95/23; 106.
carke, *v. n.* 90/51, to fret oneself.

Carons shipp, 7/13.
Catholike, a, 64 (26), 1, 9.
Cerberus, 24/17.
Ceres, 7 (3), 6; 27 (30) 1; 28 (32), 18; 43/9; 97.
Cham, 63 (23), 3, Ham.
Charites, 15/23, the Graces.
Chaucer, 3; 62/10; 71 (38), 6; 77/18; 104.
Cherill, 77/13; 82 (61), 14; 97; 104, Choerilus.
Chimera, the, 26 (28), 10, Chimer, 13, 24.
Christ, 43/18, 24; 63 (24), 1; 80 (58), 14.
Christes undivided coate, 81/14.
chuse, howe maie it, 61/18, how can it be otherwise.
Chyrill. See Cherill.
Cithereane Venus, 6 (3), 1.
Cladius Minoes, 3.
Codrus, 1.
colle, v. a. 73 (44), 4, to embrace, O. F. acoler.
cooller, sb. 17/20, colour.
Corinth, 42 (54), 7.
Corinthes, 25 (28), 5, the Corinthians.
craaking, adj. 6/16, creaking.
crag'd, adj. 44/36, rocky.
Crisopeia, 53/10; 54/21, 24, 30.
cunning, adj. 10 (7), 17, wise.
Cupid, 6 (3), 2; 7 (4), 9, 12, 20, 23; 8 (6), 9; 9/26; 33 (40), 10.
Cupido, 33 (40), 8.
curious, adj. 63 (25), 1, painstaking.
curruca, 45 (58), 3, a bird.
cutter of Queen hithe, a, 76/8.

Damasco, 25 (27), 1.
Dame Lais, 59 (13), 1.

Daphne, 85/12.
Daulian Philomell, 40 (52), 1; 103.
David, 92/10.
Dedalan bees, 49/47.
Dedalus pitt, 93/9, the Labyrinth.
Democrites, 49/53.
depainted, p. p. 10 (7), 24.
Deucalion, 39 (50), 2.
Diana, 46 (61), 1; Diane, 9 (6), 15.
Dianiane dogge, 27 (31), 1; 101.
Dictinian Diana, 8 (6), 1.
difficults, sb. 27 (30), 8, knotty points.
dispence, sb. 67 (32), 16, outlay.
Douai, 57 (8), 2.

Egerton, Sir Thomas, 1.
eise, sb. 9/21, ease.
Eldrington, 94/1.
Elios, 19 (18), 10, Helios.
endenteth with his feete, 55/25, walks on his heels?
Endore phytonesse, 95/1, pythoness.
Eneas, 5/5, 12, 27.
England, 80/2; 95/7.
entreate, v. a. 95/28, write, treat of.
enure, v. a. 14/23. "Fare il callo. Fare la piega: to make a habit, to enure."—1598; Florio.
Ephereian Lais, 41 (54), 2. Ephyra was another name for Corinth.
Ephrosine, 14 (13), 19.
Epidaure, 16 (14), 1, 7, 11.
Ethnicks, 11/1, 13; 81 (59), 11, heathen.
Euphemen, 34 (41), 4, 7, 9.
Eurinome, 14/2.
Europa, 85 (66), 7.

INDEX. 109

extremities, *sb.* 47/19, extravagance.

Fames horse, 26/22.
faulting, *adj.* 78 (54), 4, defaulting.
fellowe like, *adj.* 33/4, as a comrade.
fett, *v. a.* 7/18, fetch.
ffee, *sb.* 68 (33), 1, fief.
filius ante patrem, 86 (67), 9, a herb.
Flaccus. *See* Horace.
fleete, *v. n.* 9/8, to flit.
flienge, *pres. p.* 9/21, fleeing.
flitt, *v. a.* 12 (10), 22, to abandon.
force, *sb.* 55/31, effect.
forcinge, not, *pres. p.* 77 (52), 4, not caring.
for why, 86 (68), 9, wherefore.
Francis George, 81 (60), 7, 13; 105.
frise, *v. n.* 7 (3), 8, freeze.
frise clothed frut, 43 (56), 4.
frowinced, *adj.* 42 (54), 9, wrinkled.
fyle, *v. a.* 65/18, to defile.

Ganymede, 29 (34), 3; 36 (45), 4, 7.
Garrett, 75 (47), 15.
Gascoigne, 62/11; 104.
Gebers cooke, 96/27; 106.
glasse perspective, *sb.* 62 (21), 4, a telescope.
glose, *v. n.* 90/46, to flatter.
glosinge, *adj.* 89/23, flattering.
glose, *v. a.* 13/24, to gloss or comment.
Gorgon, the, 60 (17), 4.
Gorgon horse, 17/15, Pegasus.
Goulding, 77/16; 104.
Greece, 5/2.

Gretiane, 17/2.
guelye, *adj.* 38/5, red, from gules.

Halcyon daies, 28 (32), 19; 101.
halse, *v. a.* 85 (66), 9, to embrace.
halsing, *pres. p.* 14/12. A.S. *hals*, the neck.
hante, *v. a.* 90/79, to haunt, frequent.
Heliotropium, 19/2, 9.
Hercules, 24/1, 27.
Herseus, 85/13, Herse.
heste, *sb.* 77 (51), 5, command. A.S. *hæs*.
heysuge, 45 (58), 4, hedge-sparrow.
hier, *sb.* 22 (22), 3, rental; derived from hiring out or letting his land.
Holborne hill, 67/1; 104.
Homer, 57 (9), 5.
Horace, 1; 41 (52), 12; 82 (61), 11.
hornifie, *v. a.* 86/18, to cuckold.
Hunslowe downe, 80 (58), 3, Hounslow Heath, Middlesex.

Iacchus, 7 (3), 6.
India, 19/1.
Ingland. *See* England.
inures. *See* enure.
Italians, the, 82 (60), 12.
itterating, in, gerund, 3, in repeating. "This is the very cause why we *iterate* the Psalms oftner than any other part of Scripture besides.'—Hooker, *Eccl. Pol.*, bk V., p. 238, ed. 1676.

Jack, 76 (49), 1.
Jesse, 53 (1), 3.
Jewes, the, 43/15, 25.
John, 73 (43), 1.
John, St, 92/29.

110   INDEX.

Jove, 14/2 ; 16 (15), 2 ; 29 (34), 4, 13 ; 30 (36), 11 ; 32 (38), 1, 23 ; 32 (39), 1 ; 33 (40), 7 ; 36 (45), 4 ; 40 (51), 2 ; 43 (56), 1 ; 43 (57), 1 ; 46 (61), 10 ; 58/13 ; 60 (16) 3 ; 61 (18), 2, 9 ; 81 (60), 9 ; 85 (66), 6.
Jove his swayne, 40 (50), 10, the eagle.
joyce, *sb.* 27 (30), 4, juice.
Judea, 53 (1), 1 ; 104, Judah.
Juno, 26 (29), 11 ; 43 (57), 3.
Juvenall, 1.

Kate, 72 (42), 1.
keepe, take noe k. of, *v. a.* 91/88, take no heed of.
kinde, *sb.* 12 (10), 22 ; 15/13 ; 32/10 ; 83 (64), 3 ; 85 (66), 8, nature.

leaste, *conj.* 42 (53), 13, unless, except.
Leucosia, 44/16.
Ligia, 44/15.
lins, *v. n.* 73 (43), 6, ceases. See index to *The Times' Whistle*, E. E. T. S., *s. v.* Linne.
Lisander, 2.
London, 80 (58), 10.
losse, *adj.* 12/6, loose.
Lucas Contiles, 3.
Lucifer, 33 (40), 15.
lune, *sb.* 92/26, Luna, i. e. silver.

Mars, 28/21 ; 53/17 ; 54 (3), 3 ; 85 (66), 8, 9.
Mars his blowe, 16/9.
Martine, Martinus, 71 (39), 1, 2, 5.
Maya, 85/14.
maye game, a, 61 (19), 5.
meane, the, 41 (52), 6, moderation.

meane, *sb.* 54/26, help. " I pray you be my *mean* To bring me where to speak with Madam Silvia."—*T. Gent. of V.*, I. iv. 13—14.
Medusa, 26/15 ; 101.
Meering, 61 (19), 1.
melitane dogge, the, 23 (25), 1 ; 98.
Mercurie, 8 (5), 2 ; 15/43 ; 22/16 ; 37/18, 23 ; 85/13.
Mercurie, *sb.* 92/26, quicksilver.
messe, *sb.* 67/1, a party. " A *mess* of Russians left us but of late."—*Love's Labour Lost*, V. ii. 361.
Metamorphoses, the, of Ovid referred to, 86 (68), 2.
Mevius, 1.
mich, 21/21, much.
Minerve, dissyllable, 22/15, Minerva, 37/24 ; 40/6 ; 53/17.
Momus, 6/12 ; 71/11.
mongers, 67/1, traders. A.S. *mangere.*
Moses, 81 (60), 1.
mowes, *v. n.* 69/18, makes faces. Fr. *moue.*
Myrtilus, 21 (21), 1, 16.

Nero, 5/20.
Nestor, 7/20.
note, *v. a.* 44/34, denote.

orient, most, *adj.* 16/6, luxuriant ?
Ovid, 58/17 ; 82/9 ; 86 (68), 1 ; 104.
Oxford, 57 (8), 2.

Pallas, 26 (29), 9 ; 32/9, 23 ; 40/6 ; 48/19.
parasite smell-feast, the, 58 (11), 5.
Paris, 26/1.
Paris [the city], 57 (8), 2.

INDEX. 111

Parthenos, 44/15.
Paulus Jovius, 3.
Pawle [St], 60 (16), 5.
Pegase, Pegas, dissyllables, 16 (15), 4; 26/19.
Pegasus, 26 (28), 14.
Pegasine horse, 17/25.
Penelope, 49/10.
Perithous, 77/20.
Perseus, 1, Persius the satirist.
Perseus. *See* Pretus.
Perseus, 60 (17), 2.
Peter, St, 86 (68), 9, 23.
peyse, *sb.* 27 (30), 9, poise, balance.
Phebee, 46 (61), 8, the moon.
Phœbus or Phebus, 8 (6), 2; 19/5, 14; 29 (35), 2; 37 (47), 2; 49/47; 85/10.
Phœbus fier, 21 (22), 1, the sun.
Philopolites, 93/13, loving one's fellow-citizens.
Pitacus, 85/43; 105.
pluritane, a, 59 (13), 4.
Pluto, 11/15; 21 (20), 13; 28/1, 13; 71 (40), 3, 8.
Polipus, 39/7, a fish.
port, 90/68, bearing, behaviour.
portrait, *v. a.* 93/14, portray. "I labour to *pourtraict* in Arthure, before he was king, the image of a brave knight."—Preface to the *Fairie Queene*.
presse, *sb.* 91/89, crowd.
preste, *adj.* 84/34, ready.
Pretus, 25 (28), 1; 41 (53), 3.
Priam, 5/4.
Prometheus, 32 (39), 3.
Protestant, a, 64 (26), 1.
Proteus, 34 (42), 2, 13.

quintessence, 67 (32), 14. "Essentia Quinta [with Chymists],
quintessence, i. e. the 5th essence, a medicine made of the most powerfully working and acting particles of its ingredients."—*Bailey's Dict.*, Vol. II.

raughte, *p. p.* 7 (4), 10, seized. See *Hen. VI.*, pt. 2, II. iii. 43.
rede, *sb.* 21 (20), 13, counsel.
Remora, 29 (33), 1; 102, a fish.
retayne, *v. n.* 53/10, be a follower of. "To *Reteyne* to one, attingere ad aliquem."—*Levins*.
ride, *v. a.* 90/47, deride.
ridinge rime, 77/15.
ripier, *sb.* 76 (49), 2, a hawker of fish. Spelman says the name is derived from the basket in which the fish is brought to market, anglice, a ripp.
roaging beggar, the, 58 (11), 4.
Romans, the, 48/15.
Rose, the, within Newgate, 75/1, a tavern.
rosiall faces, 14/7.

Salamanca, 57 (8), 1.
Sardanapalus, 12/5.
Satan, 81/13.
Satans gayle [jail], 11/19.
Saturn, 29/11; 43 (57), 1; 85 (66), 1.
Saturns cursed starr, 61/7.
sawes, *sb.* 56 (5), 7, sayings.
Saxons, the, 81 (59), 1.
Scilla, Scylla, or Silla, 1, Sulla.
Scismatikes referred to, 81 (59), 6.
seche, *v. a.* 16 (14), 2, seek.
Seneca, 12 (11), 1.
Sisiphus, 96/23.
sister twinned, *adj.* 14/8.
shadowes, *v. n.* 84/10, forebodes?
shamefastnes, 84/26, modesty.

INDEX.

skande, *p. p.* 81 (60), 11, understood.
slater, *sb.* 26/15, slaughter.
Smirnians, the, 10 (7), 17.
Socrates, 13/1.
Sol, *sb.* 92/26, gold.
Solomon, 94/2, 7.
Spencer, 71 (38), 1.
springes, *sb.* 22 (23), 7, weeds.
sprite, 81 (60), 1, inspiration.
sprite, 95/3, ghost.
squamous, *adj.* 44/7, scaly.
stickler, *sb.* 84/8. A stickler interposed between combatants, who had fought long enough, with a stick. The word occurs in *Troilus and Cressida*, V. viii. 18.
Strymonian cranes, 39 (50), 1.
Stukelie, 71 (40), 1, 7.
Synon, 5/1.
Syrens, the, 43 (57), 4, 6, 24, 27, 30, 37.

Talmud, the, referred to, 82 (60), 13.
Taurus hill, 39 (50), 5.
Telemachus, 49/8.
terene, *adj.* 24/23, earthly.
Terminus, 30 (36), 3, 9; 103.
Tetragramaton, 93/35. The four letters of the name Jehovah in Hebrew.
Thalia, 14 (13), 17.
Thesius, 77/20.

Thetis bedd, 18/11, the sea.
th'ye, 83 (62), 7, the eye.
Tiberius, 10/2.
Tibullus, 82 (61), 12.
Topas, Sir, 3, 77/15; 82 (61), 14.
Troy, 5/3, 12, 29.
Tullie, 36 (46), 6.

Ulisses, 49/9.
ure, *sb.* 28 (31), 20; 62 (21), 1, use.

Valence, Mr Thomas, 47 (63), 1; 103.
vawted, *adj.* 38/10, vaulted.
vegitive, *adj.* 42 (52), 6, vegetable.
Venus, 6/7, 15; 7 (4), 10; 12/12; 14/3; 26 (29), 7; 54 (3), 1; 85 (66), 9; 94/11.
Venus bande, 12/18, Venus's fetters.
Venus squire, 93/2, Bacchus.
vilde, *p. p.* 30 (35), 7, reviled.
Virgill, 1, 82/8.
Vulcan, 32/7; 41 (51), 2.

wales, 5/3, walls.
Will, 76/3, 13.
Willford, 73 (44), 1.
Windsore, 80/1.
wynne, *v. n.* 71 (39), 3, ween, think.

Zoilus, 71/10.

The manufacturer's authorised representative in the EU for product safety is Oxford University Press España S.A. of El Parque Empresarial San Fernando de Henares, Avenida de Castilla, 2 - 28830 Madrid (www.oup.es/en or product.safety@oup.com). OUP España S.A. also acts as importer into Spain of products made by the manufacturer.
Printed and bound by CPI Group (UK) Ltd, Croydon, CR0 4YY

20/03/2026

02075337-0010